T0311822

Cambridge Elements ≡

Elements in Global Urban History
edited by
Michael Goebel
Graduate Institute Geneva
Tracy Neumann
Wayne State University
Joseph Ben Prestel
Freie Universität Berlin

CITIES AND NEWS

Lila Caimari
CONICET

CAMBRIDGE
UNIVERSITY PRESS

CAMBRIDGE
UNIVERSITY PRESS

University Printing House, Cambridge CB2 8BS, United Kingdom

One Liberty Plaza, 20th Floor, New York, NY 10006, USA

477 Williamstown Road, Port Melbourne, VIC 3207, Australia

314–321, 3rd Floor, Plot 3, Splendor Forum, Jasola District Centre,
New Delhi – 110025, India

103 Penang Road, #05–06/07, Visioncrest Commercial, Singapore 238467

Cambridge University Press is part of the University of Cambridge.

It furthers the University's mission by disseminating knowledge in the pursuit of education, learning, and research at the highest international levels of excellence.

www.cambridge.org
Information on this title: www.cambridge.org/9781108823807
DOI: 10.1017/9781108914666

First published 2022

A catalogue record for this publication is available from the British Library.

ISBN 978-1-108-82380-7 Paperback
ISSN 2632-3206 (online)
ISSN 2632-3192 (print)

Cities and News

Elements in Global Urban History

DOI: 10.1017/9781108914666
First published online: February 2022

Lila Caimari
CONICET

Author for correspondence: Lila Caimari, lilacaimari@gmail.com

Abstract: This Element examines urban imaginaries during the expansion of international news between the late nineteenth and the early twentieth centuries, when everyday information about faraway places found its way into newspapers all over the world. Building on the premise that news carried an unprecedented power to shape representations of the world, it follows this development as it made its way to regular readers beyond the dominant information poles, in the great port-cities of the South American Atlantic. Based on five case studies of typical turn-of-the-century foreign news, Lila Caimari shows how current events opened windows onto distant cities, feeding a new world horizon that was at once wider and eminently urban.

Keywords: journalism, press, global news, urban imaginaries, South American history

ISBNs: 9781108823807 (PB), 9781108914666 (OC)
ISSNs: 2632-3206 (online), 2632-3192 (print)

Contents

1 Cityscapes in the Age of Global News

Out in the Argentine Pampas, in February of 1905, two *gauchos* talk about the week's events. While sharing a *mate*, one of them remarks upon the names of Russian cities appearing in the "Telegrams" section of the newspaper: Sebastopol, Moscow, Saint Petersburg. "Such beautiful names of cities and towns," his friend Don Pedro responds. He goes on to say that they sound upper-class. Everyone there must be "bourgeois." The names also remind him of aromatic drinks, or cosmetic powders. One could search the Pampas in vain for similar sounds, he laments. The names of *criollo* towns cannot compare with those of such refined, faraway cities. His friend disagrees. There's nothing wrong with *criollo* names, he says. This land is generous. There's nothing to complain about. And, after all, "What do you know about those places?"[1]

Published in the popular magazine *PBT* in Buenos Aires, this parody was directed at the many casual conversations triggered among local readers by news from distant cities. Of course, those readers were heavily concentrated in large towns, but the expansion of international content was such that it was humorously assumed to reach even those rural characters who were expected to know the least about the outside world. *Cities and News* looks at this exhilarating and confusing moment when glimpses of distant urban centers became an everyday occurrence thanks to structural changes in the way information was produced and made available. It does so based on a general premise: at the turn of the twentieth century, the triumph of news as the organizing principle of content played an important part in shaping the notions of the world offered to readers, and this world had a heavy urban slant.

The intersection between the urban environment and modern journalism has long been understood in all its meaningfulness. The much-grown metropolis of the late nineteenth century was the chief producer of news. Cities were the stage for politics, where the main public figures had their base and where institutions provided a window through which to follow debates and the spectacle of power struggles. Even if there was a war happening somewhere in the open fields, the main news about it was produced in the city, which reflected heavily upon the news itself. The city was also the natural environment of social and cultural life, with theater seasons providing a popular feature of coverage, and burgeoning literary circuits offering a home for those interested in poetry and fiction (including many journalists working on modern newspapers). Ballrooms, parks and racetracks were other stages for the wealthy and fashionable, while the poor concentrated in great numbers in other areas of the same cities. Indeed,

---

[1] *PBT*, February 4, 1905, p. 32. The term *gaucho* refers to rural cowboys from the South American Pampas.

the large city of the industrial era was an experiment in the coexistence of different social and ethnic groups, as well as, ultimately, a place of conflict and violence. There was political violence, to be sure – riots and incidents between citizens and state forces, for example. And there was also much accidental violence, with fires suddenly raging in precarious buildings and motor vehicles creating new dangers in the streets. It is little surprise that newspapers sprang up at the core of many great cities across the world, where reporters could capture such a wealth of attractive information for an ever-growing reading public, and reflect the chaos and density of urban life, becoming a crucial part of its fabric in the process. As the work of Chicago School pioneer Robert Park showed early on, the study of the urban environment can hardly be separated from that of the press: the newspaper is where the city was first written – the privileged place that encrypted modern urban daily life.[2]

Analyses of the multiple intersections of the city and the press have underscored the symbolic power of this medium and how it demarcated so many dimensions of everyday life for those who lived between the 1800s and the 1900s. Creating mental itineraries, defining ideas of danger and security, distinguishing zones as legible and illegible, healthy or unhealthy: the capacity of the modern press to produce hierarchical and complex senses of place is one of its established features. So is its power to nourish distinctive urban identities.[3] Focusing mainly on the dominant centers of the communication system – Paris, London, Berlin, New York – those studying the history of the nineteenth-century press have not generally been interested in the ability of newspapers and periodicals to produce representations of cities other than their own.[4] This feature is surprising considering that the rise of newspaper culture coincided with that of foreign correspondents, cable technologies and global news agencies. How did all this intervene in everyday representations of the city? How did new urban "scapes" – their character, their streets and forms, their luminous spaces and dark corners – find an expression? And how did these notions relate to the known world of work, social life or political participation?

Indeed, such questions have been conceptualized apropos of both urban modernity and more recent stages in the globalization of culture. Studies of

---

[2] Recent rereadings of Park's work (himself a former journalist) have emphasized the central place of journalism and communication in his sociology of the city: Martínez Gutiérrez, "Donde la ciudad se escribe"; Muhlmann and Plenel, *Le journaliste et le sociologue*.

[3] Fritsche, *Reading Berlin 1900*; Guarneri, *Newsprint Metropolis*; Kalifa et al., *La civilisation du journal*; Singer, *Melodrama and Modernity*.

[4] I refer to studies of the modern press as such, leaving aside analyses of literary fiction published in the periodical press, whose representational powers have long been acknowledged and discussed and thus provide an important framework of reference for this analysis.

the "cityscape" of the early 1900s have helped to capture the unintended and fragmented images produced by the modern urban environment, a fractured mode of representation that puzzled urban theorists such as Siegfried Kracauer and Walter Benjamin and was different from the intentional, artistic and continuous "landscape."[5] On a different level, the notion of "scape" captures the dissemination of such figures across distant places, and the complex process through which imagined worlds are recreated beyond national boundaries.[6] Combined with intrinsic fragmentation, then, the concept introduces the notion of large-scale movement, of mixed repertoires of images and narratives finding their way through new technologies to audiences embedded in their own contexts of meaning. Such an approach strongly resonates with changes that are at the core of nineteenth-century developments in communication. Studies on the impact of the telegraph, to mention just one example, highlight the predicament of the consumers of newspapers and magazines who decoded increasing amounts of information from faraway places, following a path that was anything but simple.[7] The capacity of the printed media to inform readers about remote locations was beyond question for those who witnessed the revolution in communications. "The world has been recently discovered for the mass of civilized mankind," observed British political economist J. A. Hobson in 1906, when referring to the facilitation of news through the press and telegraph services that had occurred in the previous years.[8] Intrinsic to this development is the broad question defined by Roger Chartier when evoking the history of globalization not only as that of an increase in circulations of goods and populations but also of the evolution of a diffuse consciousness of the world by those who remained in one place.[9]

Such an endeavor takes its cue from the significant problems raised by studies that have reflected historically on communication and sense of place.[10] In this vein, *Cities and News* adopts a hypothesis on the power of late nineteenth-century news to intervene in the construction of world horizons by creating specific scapes around information. Based on this premise, it brings the rich intersection between the press and the urban imagination closer to the complex set of variables opened by findings in the history of communication and transport networks in that period, a field that has grown remarkably in recent

---

[5] Frisby, *Cityscapes of Modernity*.

[6] First introduced in the much-evoked work of the anthropologist of contemporary globalization Arjun Appadurai, "Disjuncture and Difference in the Global Cultural Economy," the concept underlies a complex system that includes ethnoscapes, technoscapes, financescapes, media-scapes and ideoscapes.

[7] Carey, *Communication as Culture*, p. 21.

[8] Quoted in Bell, "Cyborg Imperium, c. 1900," pp. 50–52.

[9] Chartier, "La conscience de la globalité. Commentaire."

[10] Rantanen, "The New Sense of Place in 19th Century News."

years.[11] It assumes that the new distribution of information amplified and diversified the universe of representations, expanding the spectrum of topics and ranges used to describe the city. In this context, it observes the ways in which the increasing priority of news as press content – at the expense of opinion columns or literary fiction, for example – provided a selective principle for graphic and narrative materials, turning the urban milieu into a more or less explicit presence around many topics – festivities, funerals, wars, revolutions, natural disasters. The expansion of international "current events" had the effect of reorganizing urban repertoires: feeding ideas about which cities constituted "the world," about their general outlook and, by extension, about the reader's own urban setting.

To observe this transformation, our point of view will be the Atlantic seaboard of South America, with the primary focus on Buenos Aires, the region's main press market, where newspapers and magazines displayed a highly ambitious informative scope. Distant from the dominant poles of the global network (London, Paris), the Argentine capital was at the same time intensely connected. Its inhabitants were immersed in a teeming media ecology, in which the effects of the communications revolution were felt with particular intensity. News from afar worked its way into local frameworks of heterogeneous meanings, often requiring a great deal of artifice to ensure even the most basic effectiveness. As we shall see, the weight of the distance separating these communities of readers from the events in question would manifest itself in various ways, but especially in the lag time between physical and telegraphic circulation, putting into stark relief the persistence of geography.

Questions about the integration of Latin American societies into the world – and the world into Latin American societies – are very old indeed, and have been at the heart of global history long before it acquired that name. In fact, they have inspired a vast tradition of studies interested in the first contacts with Spain and Portugal in the early sixteenth century, the development of a specific type of economic relationship with Europe and the intricate process of cultural hybridization that resulted.[12] This long, sinuous path was disrupted during the early

---

[11] Born from ground-breaking studies such as Daniel Headrick's *The Invisible Weapon*, this field is today much developed thanks to a growing wealth of research providing critical insights into the hidden mechanisms of late 1800s communication and the circulation of information on a global scale. Several studies will be evoked as their specific contributions become relevant to this reconstruction. A useful essay on the North Atlantic cable system is Müller's, "From Cabling the Atlantic to Wiring the World." Substantive additions to this burgeoning field include Osterhammel's, *The Transformation of the World*, pp. 710–722; and Wenzlhuemer, *Connecting the Nineteenth-Century World*.

[12] On the singular path of Latin American historiography toward global history, see Sergio Serulnikov, "El secreto del mundo." On the potential of a Latin American perspective in the global history agenda: Conrad, Zimmermann and Scarfi, "Latin America as a Laboratory."

nineteenth-century revolutions of independence and their long wars. A new relationship with the world would be born from that process, based on notions of progress and modernity that inspired a major commitment to overseas export markets and aggressive immigration policies. The growing influence of English and (especially) French ideas, fashions and novels was seen as the cultural counterpart of this new opening to the world, displacing the references, tastes and consumption habits attached to colonial Creole-Iberian traditions.[13]

Assuming the broad strokes of this description, the following analysis works with the premise that, in urban South American societies, the understanding of this new relationship with the world went well beyond the substitution of one cultural metropolis by another. The evidence of a transformed informative environment made available to large majorities of readers suggests that greater numbers of people in Buenos Aires were beginning to make out the contours of a transformed world with a much-widened horizon that had a decidedly urban slant. This was not a rupture in itself. The development of the Spanish Empire had always had a pronounced urban tenor, as shown by the importance of its Atlantic capitals and ports, and the disproportionate influence of cities in the extended configuration of the map of Latin American culture.[14] At the end of the nineteenth century, when the very definition of the world was being redrawn by the intersection of a new logic of communication with local criteria of relevance, that focus would remain concentrated on large cities, albeit in a rapidly expanding repertoire.

By putting attention on the incidence of news in this process, this exercise also seeks to engage in a dialogue with the history of South American cultural imaginaries, thus complementing the current trend of research developed within the frame of intellectual history and literary studies. In recent years, much attention has been paid to a perspective of "networks," drawing a map of previously ignored links between the region's capitals and those in the north, and also between cities within the region. A vast array of personal epistolaries, international conferences, reciprocal visits, bilateral projects and expanded diplomacy, and the new digital access to the body of correspondences and publications that accompanied these circulations, has established beyond any doubt the density of the relational fabric among the region's late nineteenth-century elites. Meanwhile, a vast area of studies has developed around nineteenth-century travel writings and a few eminent newspaper correspondents. One by one, the addition of these threads has broadened narratives of cultural modernization.[15]

---

[13] The best synthesis of this fundamental process remains Tulio Halperin Donghi's *The Contemporary History of Latin America*.

[14] On this point, see Romero's masterful *Latinoamérica. Las ciudades y las ideas*, pp. 10–22.

[15] This description suits a large portion of current studies on Latin American intellectual and cultural history as is evident from programmes in the much-expanded conferences on Latin

This study builds upon and hopes to complement that point of view by pointing to the power of news in the making of a South American world horizon made available to the great majority, while paying more than the usual attention to the intervening (material) paths of the written word and the printed image. It adopts Park's classic definition of news as an alternative (but widely available) source of knowledge. A short and independent unit of communication that can be easily comprehended, news is essentially transient and ephemeral and, as such, devoid of context other than that required to make it comprehensible and interesting. Despite its obvious limitations, the unsystematic and fragmentary type of knowledge produced by news is pervasive in modern societies and triggers daily conversations about the state of the world. "The typical reaction of an individual to the news is likely to be the desire to repeat it to someone," observes Park.[16] Based on the evidence of the rise of news as the primary press content, the archive underlying this project is biased toward a collection of fragmentary documents on the distant city as they provided glimpses through a prism of disparate information. This same bias will complement the available scholarship by shedding light on certain news logics that diverted attention away from the great cultural capitals of Europe, Paris in particular, showing the ways in which other cities – some very distant; others closer to home – also fitted into the picture of the "world."

This cultural history of news seeks to avoid a naïve vision of the rules underlying the system of information that supplied newspapers and magazines in cities that were eccentric to the global metropoles of communication. It assumes that the content agenda was shaped by forces in which each instance (newspaper, journalist, news, cable companies) participated with unequal power. Likewise, it assumes that geographic location established possibilities and impossibilities that were difficult to reverse. Nevertheless, it attempts to move the scope of analysis beyond a linear history of domination (or of resistance to domination), or the economic and political history of its material basis. As Thérenty and Vaillant assert, even in the case of press circulation between metropoles and colonies, the effects resembled appropriation and hybridization more than they did domination, a distinction that is even more relevant in contexts outside of colonial systems.[17] Moreover, it has been clearly demonstrated that communications infrastructures originally built for specific

---

American Intellectual History and the contents of the chief journals in the field, such as *Prismas. Revista de Historia Intelectual* (Bernal, Universidad de Quilmes). In the past years, important collections of travel writing edited and annotated by high-quality scholars have flourished. Several authors will be evoked in these pages for the specific contributions of their work.

[16] Park, "News as a Form of Knowledge."

[17] Thérenty and Vaillant, *Presse, nations et mondialisation au xixe siècle*, p. 9.

purposes (war, imperial control, financial development) did not necessarily (or exclusively) generate the kind of content they were designed for. Indeed, the evidence points to a system that was polymorphous and heterogeneous, with ample room for autonomous development and unforeseen results.[18]

What follows is an analysis of news circulating across vast distances, and opening windows onto remote cities. Rather than approaching this picture through one exhaustive case study of reception, a set of five distinct news events is evoked, all originating in cities far from Buenos Aires: Rio de Janeiro, Monza, Beijing, Saint Petersburg and Valparaiso. While well aware of the sacrifice this choice entails in terms of extensive, fully detailed analysis of each case, it hopes to highlight the wide-ranging effects of the information network at the peak of its capacity, as well as the varied, fragmented horizon that it created. Cases have been selected to reflect a range of news that was typical of this period – state funerals, presidential visits, imperial wars, social revolutions, natural catastrophes – and which involved cities that owed their visibility to the emerging journalistic logic. *Cities and News* will observe how local appropriations of distant events contributed to the construction of a new world-horizon, as well as the ways in which this construct became intertwined with the everyday experience of readers as they turned to newspapers and magazines for information, opinion, advice and entertainment – just like those imaginary *gauchos* chatting about the news from Sebastopol or Saint Petersburg.

2 News of the World

In early 1849, the journalist and writer Domingo F. Sarmiento (1811–1888) complained in a newspaper in Santiago de Chile about the isolation that prevented him from reading the press from other countries. Recently returned from a trip to France and the United States, he compared the situation in the city of his political exile with that of the American ports of the North Atlantic, which received "enormous quantities of up-to-date newspapers and periodicals" by steamer.[19] Why could Chileans not enjoy the same access to the written word? Sarmiento grumbled about the reasons: the anachronistic sailing ships, archaic bureaucracy and, more generally, a number of geographical, political and economic factors that held up the delivery of printed material for months, depriving Chile of the kind of circulation that, in his opinion, was one of the distinguishing characteristics of civilization.

The young Sarmiento was tireless in the pursuit of his goals – and was rather exaggerated in the picture of isolation he painted, as recent studies have

---

[18] Nikkles, *Under the Wire*, pp. 79–103; Britton, *Cables, Crises and the Press.*
[19] "Correo," *La Crónica,* 1 April 1849 in Sarmiento, *Obras Completas*, Vol. X, p. 94.

shown.[20] With an entire life and career before him, there would be ample time for other great journeys, to return to his native Argentina and be elected president and to use the power of that office to initiate major policies and projects, beginning with immigration, education, transportation and communications. Throughout this trajectory, he would remain in close contact with the city of his exile, so he would also have time to see changes in Santiago de Chile's relationship with the world. The laconic, self-absorbed society he had criticized so vehemently began to embrace subscription to press publications from other countries far beyond what he could have imagined in those early years.[21]

It may be that this change did not appear as great to Sarmiento as it really was, since he would follow the progress from Buenos Aires, where he lived during his years of maturity and greatest political activity. In that great South Atlantic port, the press (local and imported) was, in the 1880s, accessible to a wide range of readers, in numbers that clearly exceeded those of the literate elite. Since the early years of the century, in fact, ships dispatched from ports in the northern hemisphere had been delivering books, newspapers and magazines, and the pace of these deliveries had only grown. Imperfect as they are, the numbers reported by the (then) nascent national Post Office provide an outline of the growth in the last decades of the century. The 300,000 parcels of printed matter unloaded in 1879 had risen to one and a half million in 1887, shortly before Sarmiento's death. By 1896, it had grown to three and a half million, and then more than eight and a half million in 1900.[22] This growth greatly exceeded the (also extraordinary) rise in the city's population, which nearly tripled (from 286,000 to 649,000) between 1880 and 1895 as a result of European immigration, reaching one and a half million in 1914.[23] If we assume that about three-quarters of that printed material remained in the city (as the Post Office numbers indicate), and that approximately two-thirds of the contents of those mail-bags were periodicals (as the statistics on reception by category suggest), this means

---

[20] On the regional circulation of letters and prints during the Chilean anti-Rosista exile: Blumenthal, *Exile and Nation-State Formation in Argentina and Chile, 1810–1862*, pp. 85–125. On access to European ideas: Jaksic, "Disciplinas y temáticas de la intelectualidad chilena en el siglo XIX," pp. 23–42.

[21] Caimari, "La carta y el paquete."

[22] The data used in this section come from the statistics of the Union Postale Universelle, *Statistique Générale, Service Postal publiées par le Bureau International* (Bern: Imprimerie Suter & Lierow, 1887–1900). Although not always consistent in the definition of categories, this information is congruent with the annual statistics of the Argentine Postal Office. Since this agency's monopoly on these circulations was not absolute, these are approximate figures intended to provide general trends. From the 1880s onwards, UPU statistics include books and newspapers in the same "printed" category, but projections of previous dates suggest that about two-thirds of the total were periodicals. Caimari, "Derrotar la distancia."

[23] Devoto, "La inmigración."

that, at the turn of the century, Buenos Aires was absorbing about eighteen million copies a year, equivalent to twenty-seven copies of imported periodicals per capita, far more than the one copy per inhabitant seen two decades earlier. At the turn of the century, Argentina was the fourth country in the world in terms of per capita circulation of letters and printed matter, according to the Universal Postal Union (UPU).[24]

To a lesser extent, other cities in the region participated in the same phenomenon, since, on the way to Buenos Aires, those ships also unloaded many bags in other ports, such as Montevideo and Rio de Janeiro.[25] In the span of a single lifetime, these capitals' relationships with the world had changed completely. With differences according to each case, the data describe a very clear evolution: from the middle of the century onwards, and with gathering intensity, imported printed goods were becoming a widely accessible product. The evidence indicates that the distribution of these shipments was uneven, and that the bulk made it only as far as the larger cities, namely, those linked to the port systems and the networks of global circulation: Santiago and Valparaiso in Chile, Montevideo in Uruguay, Buenos Aires in Argentina, Rio de Janeiro and São Paulo in Brazil.

To what extent did this access represent a change in societies where news from Europe had always been at the center of the diet of information? Born as the ports and capitals of the Ibero-American colonial system, these cities (which were only recently becoming large urban centers) had been marked by the extreme distance from their metropoles, and by a certain cultural and linguistic homogeneity. For three centuries, news from Madrid and Lisbon had been arriving with delays of two to three months. At the beginning of the nineteenth century, these materials reached their consumers along with news provided by epistolary correspondence, all of them read in sporadic waves following the rhythm of the shipping schedules, with full awareness of the temporal (spatial) gap that separated them from their origin. After independence, in the 1810s and 1820s, these cities' growing integration with the world would still bear traces of this relationship, with informational remittances maintaining the long cultural link with distant Europe. On the level of ideas, this link increasingly identified with England and France, leading to more interest in what was published there. Thus, before the great rise in the scale of circulation and the expansion of the press markets, the media economies of the early 1800s were nurturing an informed reading public interested in whatever news (political and economic, but also aesthetic and philosophical) came from European capitals.[26]

---

[24] Argentine Republic, *Memoria del Ministerio del Interior*, 1900, p. 93.

[25] On French periodicals in Rio de Janeiro: Guimarães, "From Liner to Telegraph."

[26] Goldgel, *Cuando lo nuevo conquistó América*, pp. 47–108.

Overlayed on this old predisposition were new factors that, with the advance of the century, led to concrete shifts in expectations regarding access to these goods. One important dimension spoke to the interests of economic elites, as they were attracted by the promise of a radical reformulation in which steam and telegraph technologies would reconfigure the rules of access to overseas markets in economies that were resolutely turning to international trade. Another element had to do with the expansion of European immigrant communities, a fact that would profoundly modify the universe of readers – first in Buenos Aires and Montevideo, then in São Paulo, and in dozens of small and medium-sized cities in their areas of influence. All of them would see, in the last two decades of the century, the emergence of high concentrations of recent arrivals, most of them from Mediterranean countries. In 1900, the Italian community of Buenos Aires was larger than that of the ten largest cities in the United States combined. São Paulo, Montevideo and Rosario each had more Italians than any North American city outside of New York. Immigrants from Spain were, in cities of the Argentine and Uruguayan Pampas, only slightly fewer.[27] This unique demographic shift would give birth to complex, hybrid cultures, in highly urbanized societies with distinct modern features. Indeed, the area comprising Southern Brazil, Uruguay and the Argentine Pampas has been considered to be a transnational region in itself, and it happens to coincide with some of the most developed publishing markets, the highest literacy rates and the latest infrastructure for connectivity with the outside world.[28]

By the century's end, those widely spaced shipments of press and correspondence had become a steady stream of packages containing major newspapers, illustrated magazines, pieces on the latest Parisian fashion, literary and scientific periodicals, socialist and anarchist tracts, and much more. The expansion of the Hispanic and Luso-American market in the last three decades of the century was so enormous, in fact, that it would become a coveted horizon for publishers beyond Spain and Portugal, resulting in an important rise in the publishing industry in Spanish and Portuguese in France, with the participation of shipping companies capable of delivering their products to those distant ports.[29]

Paradoxically, by the end of the century the availability of European printed matter had ceased to be as decisive as the young Sarmiento had imagined. By

---

[27] Moya, "Migration and the Historical Formation of Latin America in a Global Perspective," 48.

[28] Goebel, *Overlapping Geographies of Belonging*.

[29] Cooper-Richet, "La presse hispanophone parisienne au XIX siècle"; Fernández, "El monopolio del mercado internacional de impresos en castellano en el siglo XIX"; Barbier, "Le commerce international de la librairie française au XIXe siècle (1815–1913)." On the production of printed goods for the Brazilian market: Mollier, "Introduction," p. 12.

then, the imported press was just one of many options in a broader local offering. The history of the expansion and modernization of the South American press is similar in its general lines to that of other cities in the nineteenth century, where the increase in literacy rates, urbanization and growing interconnection converged in the unprecedented development of this market. As in other cities, there was a diversification of formats, a multiplication of print runs, a broadening of the thematic and expressive spectrum and a growing professionalization of journalism.[30] The process would also increase the incidence of newspapers in daily life. Organizing time, constructing social identities, describing the urban environment and its inhabitants: a whole "civilization" was linked to the press. Never before (and never after) would it be so important in the lives of so many.[31]

Varying in timing and scale, the press cycles in South American cities would follow similar paths, gaining momentum in the last two decades of the century in cities marked by export expansion and greater political stabilization in the region. The focus of this study will be on Buenos Aires, which was the most prosperous and most populated city at the time, and the primary press market in the region. Buenos Aires exhibited unusually high literacy rates (around 70 percent in 1895, and almost 80 percent in 1914) as a result of very consistent educational policies.[32] It should not be surprising then that the largest number of press titles was concentrated there (some 279 in 1896, half of those published domestically) or that those titles were so stable. Distributed in the streets, bars, workshops, clubs and homes, this corpus included many newspapers (twenty-eight in 1896), among them the two most ambitious and powerful in South America, *La Prensa* and *La Nación*, with print runs in the tens of thousands. At the turn of the century, *La Prensa* surpassed the hundred thousand mark. Besides daily newspapers, a wealth of other periodicals nourished readers' interests in more segmented ways, with a strong satirical press, numerous illustrated magazines and a plethora of literary, fashion, educational, economic, theatrical, scientific and professional offerings.[33]

---

[30] The great cycle of modernization is a structuring dimension in the history of the nineteenth-century press. By way of example: Schudson, *Discovering the News*; Guarneri, *Newsprint Metropolis*; Charle, *Le siècle de la presse (1830–1939)*; Barnhust and Nerone, *The Form of News*.

[31] Kalifa et al., *La civilisation du journal*, pp. 7–21.

[32] These rates were always considerably higher than those in the rest of the country, with gaps of up to 30 percentage points. Di Pietro and Tófalo, *La situación educativa a través de los censos de población*.

[33] A catalogue of available periodicals in Buenos Aires in 1896 in: Navarro Viola, *Anuario de la prensa argentina*. On the modernization of the *Porteño* press: Checa Godoy, *Historia de la prensa Iberoamericana*, pp. 222–228; Roman, "La modernización de la prensa periódica, entre *La Patria Argentina* (1879) y *Caras y Caretas* (1898)"; on the satirical press: Roman, *Prensa, política y cultura visual*.

Of the 279 Buenos Aires publications consigned in 1896, some 65 were "foreign." Immigrants interested in following current events in their land of origin, or news regarding their ethnic kin in the Americas, could combine reading the local newspaper with a daily in another language (English, French, Italian, Yiddish) or dozens of other periodicals related to specific regions of Spain and Italy. Twenty-two of those publications were written in Italian. In this regard, Buenos Aires represented the most notable example of a feature common to societies of the South Atlantic, where a market of inter-connected ethnic press was expanding with a focus around immigration from that country.[34]

The growing circulation of magazines and newspapers in Buenos Aires spilled across the River Plate into Montevideo, which was experiencing a parallel modernization of its own press, with twelve newspapers in 1890 and remarkable stability in the roster of titles.[35] Meanwhile, the center of the Brazilian market was well established in Rio de Janeiro. That great imperial capital, now (as of 1889) the political center of the new Republic, boasted several important dailies at the end of the century, including the veteran *Jornal do Commercio* (read by businessmen, but diversifying its contents for wider audiences), the conservative *Jornal do Brasil* (run by Rui Barbosa, a prestigious intellectual and politician), and the modern *Gazeta de Noticias*. A statistic from 1911 shows 17 newspapers in Rio, which by then had 850,000 inhabitants. The rapid rise of São Paulo at the turn of the century would create another center, one with an important Italian press and several modern papers: *O Estado de São Paulo, Correo Paulistano* and *Diario Mercantil*.[36]

In 1914, when Buenos Aires reached a million and a half inhabitants, its influence as a publishing and journalistic center was palpable throughout the region. It was not the consumption of imported press that made this difference, or the volume of postal traffic (still among the largest *per capita* in the world), but its own journalistic and editorial expansion. By then, the wide distribution of printed matter was joined by the role of its main newspapers in the information chain of cable and steam correspondents. This development took place in the context of another important trend: the expansion of international news as press content.

---

[34] Weber, "Elenco de publicaciones periódicas italianas de Buenos Aires (1854–1910)"; Galante, *Distant Loyalties*.

[35] Romano, *Revolución en la lectura*; Lobato, *Prensa obrera*. On the modernization of the press in turn-of-the century Montevideo: Checa Godoy, *Historia de la prensa Iberoamericana*, p. 189.

[36] Checa Godoy, *Historia de la prensa Iberoamericana*, p. 244; Sodré, *A história da imprensa no Brasil*, pp. 287–447; Eleutério, "Imprensa a serviço de progresso"; Barbosa, *História Cultural da Imprensa*, pp. 21–45.

At the base of this development were, of course, transformations in the sphere of transportation and communication, which redefined notions of time and distance throughout the world.[37] Anyone leafing through the newspapers in the initial stages of the "wonder" of the telegraph could see that cities connected by the wire were gaining in visibility. This manifested itself, first, on a regional scale, uniting Rio de Janeiro, Montevideo, Buenos Aires and Santiago de Chile/Valparaiso in the early 1870s.[38] In 1874, this incipient telegraphic system was linked to the global cable network, then in full expansion, accelerating the circulation of transatlantic information like never before.

Unlike other areas where this technology arrived, the cable was not conceived as a tool of colonial domination, as it was in India or Africa, for example. Rather, it was an achievement promoted and publicized by the same local elites who were driving policies of immigration, mass education and economic integration with the world.[39] Although the terms of this access were clearly different from those framing the development of the cable system in those areas, its expected effects were very similar in their linear and selective conception. "The Argentine Republic is from this day forward at the doorstep of the United States," announced Sarmiento's telegram to his counterpart Ulysses S. Grant upon the inauguration of the South Atlantic cable system.[40] As we shall see, this innovation would not produce the univocal proximity to certain points of the globe foreseen by its promoters.

Something similar can be said regarding the dream of instantaneity. As in other cities of the world, the technological wonder was described with expressions such as "the elimination of distance" and "the abolition of space" – metaphors typical of the time.[41] We will see in what ways this expectation would find concrete translation in the pages of the press. For the time being, let us establish that the implementation of the submarine cable system inaugurated a type of access to international information that would affect the news

---

[37] Wenzlhuemer, *Connecting the Nineteenth-Century World*.

[38] In addition to the abovementioned editorial market linked to steam, the rhythms and flows of information would be altered by the telegraphic connection, starting with the construction of the Montevideo–Buenos Aires cable on the bed of the River Plate in 1866. This would be followed in 1872 by the Trans-Andean line between Buenos Aires and Santiago and, shortly after, the connection of these three cities to the Brazilian ports, with their center in Rio. Until the end of the century, the submarine telegraph system was dominated by the British companies in the Pender group, which led in the cable business throughout the world, including the South Atlantic networks. From 1891, this hegemony was disputed on the Pacific Coast by the entry of American capital. Ahvenainen, *The European Cable Companies*, p. 96; Winseck and Pike, *Communication and Empire*, p. 80; Britton and Ahvenainen, "Showdown in South America."

[39] On the telegraph as an imperial tool: Headrick, *The Invisible Weapon*, pp. 50–72; on the effects of this system in Algeria: Asseraf, *Electric News in Colonial Algeria*.

[40] Quoted in: Reggini, *Sarmiento y las telecomunicaciones*, p. 185.

[41] Carey, "Technology and Ideology"; Müller, *Wiring the World*, pp. 83–118.

environment in many ways. While the circulation that was set in motion effectively accelerated the delivery of certain kinds of content, it introduced a kind of hierarchy, fragmentation and discontinuity that would have major implications for the composition of the world horizon.

In the midst of the self-celebration of such modernizing changes, newspapers were quick to emphasize what this promise entailed: connection *with Europe*, access to current events *in synchrony*. This promise was associated with another important actor: the Havas news agency, which was the first to telegraph information in the region. Based in Paris, the company soon signed contracts with dozens of newspapers on a map that replicated the design of the submarine infrastructure. As soon as the cable was inaugurated, Havas committed itself to providing a daily news service, initiating a relationship with the leading newspapers, which could, in turn, show their readers the result of this new access to the world. With more impact in some regions than in others, and in some newspapers than in others, Havas would maintain its relationship in the long term, even if the Buenos Aires press developed their own correspondent services and displaced it as the main source of telegraphic news.[42]

By the end of the century, all major newspapers had a network of exclusive correspondents in European capitals and the main cities of the region. They were a truly varied group: prestigious writers, elite travelers, scientists or artists commenting on topics of general interest. The main staple of information did not come from them, however, but from a typical figure of the increasingly news-driven dynamics of the press: the "native" contributor, paid by the piece. A more demanding sort of formal relationship connected these figures to the newspaper in question. In the late 1890s, these full-time correspondents sent out weekly reports offering a panorama of political, cultural and economic news. They were often the same individuals who sent the telegraphed daily news service. In both cases, they gathered the core of their material from the press of the city in which they were located. This practice defined a whole conception of correspondence, in which the central criterion revolved around selection, rewriting and reframing.[43]

---

[42] On the early establishment of Havas in South America: Desbordes, "Migrations and Information Networks in the 19th Century"; Desbordes, "L'information internationale en Amérique du Sud." On the place of Havas in Buenos Aires newspapers: Caimari, "De nuestro corresponsal exclusivo." On the rise of this global news market: Boyd-Barrett and Rantanen, *The Globalization of News*.

[43] Caimari, "De nuestro corresponsal exclusivo." On the emergence of the correspondent in the Buenos Aires modern press: Servelli, *A través de la República*. On the development of international correspondents in the Brazilian press: de Luca, "Correspondente no Brasil"; Rozeaux, "Être correspondant de la presse brésilienne en Europe."

In all evidence, this access to the world's current events was marked by unequal rules. The data on telegraphic circulation and tariffs, and the design of the cable infrastructure itself, speak eloquently of the power of the dominant actors in the system.[44] Within that framework, different strategies of access and circulation patterns were possible, however, and so the skills required of a foreign correspondent had to include the ability to make the most of a multi-entry system.[45] In most cases, these opportunities were to be found not on remote battlefields but in the newspapers themselves. The convention of free access to already published information was particularly profitable for these correspondents, as differences between time zones made it possible to take advantage of materials published in European morning papers. With that, and with the occasional preferential access to agency releases, a broad selection of news could be assembled to accompany the breakfast of the reader in Buenos Aires.

As the roster of correspondents diversified, and the technological conditions of transmission and transport improved, the thematic spectrum of information would expand. By the end of the century, the criteria for content admissible as "foreign" news had become much more flexible. Traces of this change can be found in all major newspapers and magazines, as well as in the instructions sent out by the large press agencies: "We are counting on you," the head of Havas told his new partners at the Associated Press in New York, "to forward it immediately to our agency in Buenos Ayres, under the direction of Buenos-Ayres-Havas, whenever a sensational event occurs anywhere in the world." These events – deaths of heads of state, revolutions, natural disasters – had absolute priority, insisted the director, head of the entire South American branch. No measures were to be spared.[46]

Among content providers both large and small, the criterion of the potential for sensation prevailed in the news hierarchy, inserting traditional political content into a framework of increasingly lax categories, which contaminated and redefined it. Distant news could speak to broad audiences, provided that it was linked to a story that made it interesting, understandable and thrilling. Thus, the international news agenda found new inflexions, at the crossroads of the sensational and the *faits divers* that sparked curiosity, empathy and amazement.

---

[44] Winseck and Pike, *Communication and Empire*, p. 147 ff.; Ahvenainen, *The European Cable Companies*, pp. 235–243.

[45] On the techniques developed by journalists working with cable news: Barth, "Making the Wire Speak."

[46] National Archives of France, Havas Fund, 5AR/113, Letter from Charles Houssaye to the Associated Press, February 18, 1902, p. 1v. Emphasis in the original. On the rise of the telegraphic *faits divers*: Palmer, *Des petits journaux aux grandes agences*, pp. 136–137.

The Places of the News

Certainly, no one would have said at the end of the century that the capitals of the South American Atlantic were disconnected from the world. With telegraphic services available in every newspaper and armies of remote correspondents sending reports and commentaries, readers had unprecedented access to the most disparate of recent events. Meanwhile, international contents also stemmed from other expanded sections of the press, such as popular fiction and advertisements.

No one could complain of isolation. In fact, more common was the opposite complaint: that an overabundance of information produced confusion and disorientation. With this came many jokes. In 1884, the satirical weekly *Don Quixote* published a false "telegraphic service" in rhyme, with local news (real or invented), from Naples, Beijing, La Plata, Marseille, Montevideo and London: the nearby and the far-flung jumbled together for the reader's enjoyment.[47] Everyone understood in a wink, since the news of the world often arrived in an unruly succession and was difficult to place in intelligible contexts. It was not always clear *here* what was happening *there*, and nagging doubts persisted about whether or not *there* was getting a clear picture of what was being transmitted from *here*. The theme of an informational "hubbub" of confusion and misunderstanding accompanied the new technology from the beginning, a symptom of persistent doubts regarding the effects of the new informational ecology.

As in other societies, skepticism was intrinsic to the rise of the telegram in Buenos Aires, so sparse and codified in its language, so devoid of context and so prone to error.[48] "We do not know if the blame belongs with correspondents, errors in transmission, clumsiness in interpretation . . ., or rather with distortion and ignorance on the part of those who interpret the telegrams transmitted to them from London," decried *La Nación* in the face of egregious errors in a transcription of news.[49] Aside from these setbacks, the proof of the technology's effectiveness was visible on the pages of newspapers and magazines that increasingly featured content from far away. Once the accuracy of the information was confirmed, the main question turned to its relevance.

Another satirical weekly, *El Mosquito*, would publish a parody of the strained readings produced by the cable news, in which ostensibly knowledgeable men would pretend to understand loose scraps of information regarding remote

---

[47] *Don Quixote,* August 31, 1884, p. 3.

[48] On the debates regarding telegraphic language in the North Atlantic cables: Müller, *Wiring the World*, pp. 120–129.

[49] *La Nación*, July 19, 1897, p. 3.

events. This was the case in a dialogue among one Don Meleagro, his wife Misia Eponina, his daughter Julia and a neighbor (Don Telésforo, who was just passing by). The head of the household read the newspaper "at his leisure, wrapped in his robe, with his cap on his head and a cigarette of dark tobacco in his mouth." When asked about the news he was reading, he replied gravely: "Telegrams from Europe, very interesting." Problems arose when others began to ask for details. Don Meleagro found it difficult to explain what he was reading. He could not decipher the news of the stock market – "I am not interested in that"; nor did he understand the politics. Neither he nor his neighbor was able to say whether the news of the blockade of the Suez Canal to Russian ships was good or bad, important or trivial, whether to take sides in the conflict and, if so, for what reasons. Also, the precise location where those events were happening was unclear:

> "Daddy," interrupts the girl Julia. "What's the Suez Canal?"
> "It's a . . . a river . . . a kind of sea over there."
> "In Russia?"
> "Yes, darling, over there. Isn't that right, Mr. Telésforo?"
> "Yes, sir."[50]

Published in 1877, when the effects of the interoceanic telegraph system were just beginning to be noticed, this parody took aim at the posture of those who read "important" news. International cables, it was understood, were not for everyone. They were intended for men of a certain position who could retire to a salon to talk about these matters while smoking cigars. At the same time, the readers of such urgent news needed to hide the fragility of their relationship with the information coming from such a prestigious source. Serious things were happening in the world. One was expected to be aware of them. The telegram carried an aura of status and urgency. But the places and characters that made up its content could also be mere passwords for an exclusive group.

Two decades later, the challenge implicit in the access to news of the world continued to raise questions. How, for example, to narrate the facts of the Anglo-Boer War, in faraway South Africa, when details of the conflict were unknown to the average reader? The illustrated magazine *Caras y Caretas* underscored the gap between the place allotted for the story and the reflections it sparked in readers in Buenos Aires.

Personal and idiosyncratic, and wholly alien to the political-military core of the conflict, each character's comments were very much situated in Buenos Aires, in settings full of recognizable details – the neighborhood bar, the downtown street, the shop counter, the armchair of a bourgeois salon. One

---

[50] *El Mosquito*, June 22, 1877, p. 1.

Image 1 ""News of the War," by Giménez; *Caras y Caretas*, March 10, 1900

after another, these scenes highlighted the contrast between the concrete experiential reality of place and the elusive abstraction of the distant news. By doing so, they pointed to an obvious problem: the news didn't work all by itself. It needed a framework of intelligibility and relevance. Communication infrastructures and news providers were not enough. Material obstacles were surmounted, but the big question of the journey of information remained. As shown in complaints and jokes, the contexts of meaning at the point of arrival would shape the effectiveness (or ineffectiveness) of each piece, so far removed from its original frame of production.

Equally decisive was the journey itself, and the range of reformulations and adaptations that took place in transit. Speaking about the flow of information in early modernity, Filippo de Vivo describes space not only as a barrier to be overcome but also as a transforming factor of information.[51] Once distance was "vanquished" by transportation and communications, the question of mediation was reopened, putting attention on the agents who intervened in the final formulation of the contents. Making the news *work* locally required selection, contextualization, segmentation, building connections with other themes . . . . Such were the central tasks of the correspondents and editors of the era. The job also fell to cartoonists, a prominent group in the periodical press, who developed their own ways of translating the crossover (through exaggeration, ridicule, paradox), taking full advantage of the collision between the "outside" news and the most stubborn of vernacular frames.

Indeed, traces of this challenge are visible in many links in the chain, since the problem went beyond the question of telegraphic lingo to touch upon larger questions of meaning, where more pieces of information made longer journeys, more quickly than ever before. Faced with this question, the Havas agency criticized newspapers that "added" details to their cables to make them more palatable in Buenos Aires.[52] Not surprisingly, then, the policy of transmitting news became increasingly restrictive so as to close off interpretation and "embroidery" as much as possible. The effectiveness and credibility of the global news were at stake. In the journey, some stories would fare better than others.

Even as they targeted errors and misunderstandings, parodies drew attention to the complexities of place composition, made necessary by information from lesser-known regions of world. New tools were introduced to complement the writing. One of these was the use of maps to accompany news of military conflicts reported in the "Exterior" section. These, in turn, were part of a more general expansion of images in the press, a development that would profoundly modify the language of information everywhere.

---

[51] De Vivo, "Microhistories of Long-Distance Information," 190.

[52] Letter from Havas-Paris to the representative in South America, Baccani, January 19, 1887; Archives Nationales de France, Havas Fund, 37 1, p. 408. The letter referred to an incident that was rather frequent: out of ignorance of context, the unfortunate intervention of a *Porteño* editor turned an act of anarchist violence into a mere *faits divers,* diverting the meaning of the transmission in the process.

In the last two decades of the century, illustration would advance as a resource in the South American daily press, accompanying varied content, and increasingly associated with current news.[53] The trend had already appeared in the "first generation" of illustrated magazines. Explanatory images were placed alongside information about the Paraguayan War (1865–70), and would become commonplace with the great expansion of information at the end of the century.[54] Part of a major shift in the visual environment, the development would be fueled by the flow of imported print, in which the genre of the "illustrated magazine" would have a prominent place. Then, at the end of the century, printed photography would change the rules of visual representation and usher in a new tool in the emerging journalistic logic connecting news and sensationalism.[55]

A crucial moment in this development was the appearance in Buenos Aires of *Caras y Caretas* (1898), a "festive, literary, artistic and current affairs" magazine. It was a turning point in the variety and ambition of the printed offering.[56] Heir to the graphic tradition of satirical magazines, *Caras y Caretas* would be a pioneer in the use of photography in mass circulation publishing. Each issue included dozens of images, provided by its own photographers (who walked the streets on the lookout for whatever might be of interest), by spontaneous contributors in the interior of the country and abroad, and through permissive attitudes regarding the reproduction of photos from imported magazines. As in so many publications around the world, the "half-tone" technique would make it possible to include photographic content in high-circulation printed matter, attracting an audience that was not always fully literate, or those who, having just disembarked from Europe, did not speak the local language. It soon became apparent that photography was extremely popular among ordinary readers. Print runs would increase exponentially. The 10,000 copies of *Caras y Caretas'* first issue became 80,000 in 1904, and 110,000 in 1910.[57]

Journalistic photography would greatly favor the consumption of international news, expanding the universe of readers far beyond the "Exterior"

---

[53] Ojeda, *La incorporación sistemática de la imagen visual a la prensa diaria argentina*.

[54] Szir, "Reporte documental, régimen visual y fotoperiodismo," 2–4. On graphic resources in satirical periodicals: Roman, *Prensa, política y cultura visual*. On the place of illustrated images in widely available printed goods in turn-of-the-century Buenos Aires: Gené and Szir, *A vuelta de página*.

[55] On the technical preconditions for this change in the printed press: Feyel, "Les transformations technologiques de la presse au XIXe siècle."

[56] Due to its importance, *Caras y Caretas* (born in Montevideo in 1890 and refounded in Buenos Aires in 1898) has been the subject of numerous studies from the literary, journalistic and graphic point of view. Rogers, *Caras y Caretas*; Romano, *Revolución en la lectura*, pp. 181–285.

[57] Szir, "El semanario popular ilustrado *Caras y Caretas*," p. 68. About photography in *Caras y Caretas*: Szir, "Entre el arte y la cultura masiva"; Tell, "Reproducción fotográfica e impresión fotomecánica."

sections of the newspapers. The image fulfilled, in this regard, a complementary function to that of the telegraphic cable: published two or three weeks later, it made visible what had only been touched upon in the daily press. The time lag between the two is a feature of the South American information system that would have consequences for graphic representation, as we shall see.

The proliferation of printed photography contributed to an environment of increasing visual density, also marked by the parallel expansion of the photo-postcard. According to data from UPU, in 1900 Argentina received some 40,000 postcards from Italy alone, while another 34,000 went to Brazil, and 2,200 to Uruguay. The number would keep growing over subsequent years, feeding an important collector's market in the process. As in other cities of the world, the production and dissemination of the photographic postcard held a fundamental place in the development of the turn-of-the-century visual culture, and in the construction of imaginaries of landscape. We shall see to what extent the new informational environment would activate postcard city-scapes as well, putting them at the service of the latest news.

Without leaving Buenos Aires, any consumer of newspapers could glean, at the very least, a vague idea of the character and landmarks of a handful of cities that there was no way of knowing directly and could compare them with what was at hand. By activating multiple resources – from the briefest of telegrams to the narrative of a high-profile correspondent, from satirical illustration to the photo postcard and photo journalism – news would be the organizing factor of a world reimagined. The following pages look at this change through a handful of paradigmatic news events of the period.

3 The News-City

Emanations of the Mourning City

Streets dotted with ribbons, crowds dressed in black following an ornate carriage in a slow caravan: the scenes follow one another, unconnected but similar. Observed by the correspondent from a balcony, by the photographer from the top of a tree or a street pole, they capture a moment of collective expression for thousands who will follow the story from afar through the newspaper's chronicle and the images of the illustrated magazine.

Few events sparked the interest of the press at the end of the nineteenth century as much as great funeral processions. The death of heads of state figured in the Havas agency's decalogue of "sensational" news, as we have seen, and, according to all evidence, the public displays around a high-profile death warranted a major deployment of resources. Of course, the scope of the report-ing was a function of the power and position of the person in question. The sumptuous funeral of Queen Victoria in February 1901 called for wider cover-age than that of other dignitaries whose deaths, like hers, were not unexpected.[58] But the lure also depended upon other factors, as shown by the attention garnered by the death of Giuseppe Verdi, whose thronging funeral processions in Milan and Rome commanded so many pages in South American cities with a strong Italian presence.[59] More importantly, the power, prestige and popular-ity of the figure in question were combined with other factors, drastically increasing the journalistic impact of a particular death. This is how the spec-tacular nature and shocking effect of the anarchist attacks at the turn of the century would transform certain funerals into massive global news events.

In Buenos Aires, there was certainly no lack of awareness of European anarch-ism. However, it was unclear how it related to actual evidence of the movement's growth in the city, and to the inevitable question of the connection between that development and the presence of so many Spanish and Italian immigrants. In a way, the "anarchist problem" was a link between Buenos Aires and those distant cities where so much news on the subject originated – Barcelona, Rome, Milan, even Saint Petersburg. But the implications of that kinship were not clear: was it possible that the violence occurring "there" might be repeated "here"? For that wide universe of readers who followed the phenomenon from a distance, news about each work stoppage and violent attack reopened the question of the nature of this diffuse, intriguing phenomenon, and the possibility that its more extreme manifestations might hit closer to home. Though that would come soon enough, there had not been any such episodes in 1900. For the moment, these concerns were driven by the international news. Meanwhile, sympathizers and activists identifying with this movement could read in the local libertarian press the latest updates and doctrinal developments in places where the European movement's base was strongest.[60] For their part, the state agents charged with monitoring and pursuing the most well-known militants maintained a police and consular network across various port cities (Marseille, Vigo, Genoa, Dunkerque), amounting to a surveillance map of popula-tion movements in the Atlantic.[61] Somehow, everyone understood that local anarchism belonged to a network that included distant cities and neighboring ports, making it one of the stranger and most disturbing manifestations of modernity in Buenos Aires.

It should come as no surprise, then, that news of the murder (in Monza on July 29, 1900) of Umberto I of Savoy, the king of Italy, caused such a stir; nor

---

[58] *Caras y Caretas*, February 23 and March 9, 1901. On press coverage of great public funerals in Argentina, see Gayol, "La unanimidad de la congoja."

[59] *Caras y Caretas*, March 9, 1901.

[60] Here I follow Albornoz, *Cuando el anarquismo causaba sensación*, pp. 29–61.

[61] Albornoz and Galeano, "Los agitadores móviles."

that the coverage led with a profile of the killer, an anarchist, and questions about the nature and morality of his beliefs. Gaetano Bresci's picture would be carried by all the major news circuits and disseminated far and wide, undergoing substantial alteration along the way. The Buenos Aires morning newspaper *La Nación*, for example, published a version of his face as imagined by the illustrator Martín Malharro based on available stories.[62] Meanwhile, there was renewed curiosity about the extent of anarchism's local reach, and whether it constituted "a link in the chain that circles the whole earth." It was concluded that the more virulent forms would not take root in Buenos Aires. The local version appeared to be a strange but harmless sect. "There is no reason for them to be bothered by the police," concluded a report.[63]

The question of the killer's motivations proved to be only one aspect of a story that would unfold gradually into others. There was that of a crime, plain and simple. Closely associated with the urban milieu, the genre of crime investigation was well-established in the press. Expanding upon resources proper to the coverage of other cases, journalists began to examine the locations of the event. Only one photograph could be connected to the attack: that of King Umberto leaving the palace on his way to a rather innocuous sporting event, where he would lose his life. Taken by a correspondent with the *Illustrated London News*, it would soon spread across the globe. Given the scarcity of documentation, *ex post facto* illustrations of the fatal scene were added, a common tool in the crime news genre. Meanwhile, the focus began to shift to the larger setting. Images of the fateful journey and the precise location of the event would soon be absorbed into a larger set of views, ultimately encompassing the city itself.[64] The anarchist attack on the king became "the tragedy of Monza," drawing attention to a beautiful Italian city, its panoramas, port, monuments, buildings, markets and squares. In the context of such an event, the urban postcard now showed the scene of a crime and invited the projection of new meanings onto the most ordinary of cityscapes. We will have the chance to see similar mutations apropos of quite disparate events. For the moment, let's note that the abrupt transformation of a town into a crime scene provided the press with a visual repertoire closely derived from the genre of the photo postcard.

Simply by virtue of its association with a homicide, any house in any neighborhood in any city might become the object of broad public scrutiny. Such was the case of the royal villa. Having now become "the home of the victim," the palace combined this common resource of the crime story with the allure of political tragedy and high-society gossip. It offered a window into

---

[62] Albornoz, *Una flor extraña*, ch. I.   [63] *Caras y Caretas*, August 11, 1900.

[64] *Caras y Caretas*, August 4, 1900; August 25, 1900; September 1, 1900. Some images of Monza published in this magazine had previously appeared in *L'Illustrazione Italiana*.

the lifestyle of the European nobility, a caste that didn't exist in the South American republics, and was therefore an object of curiosity. This vaguely *voyeuristic* interest was no doubt gratified by the views of palatial interiors, gilded halls with gargantuan chandeliers, and the ornate corridor leading to the king's chambers.[65]

Simultaneous and fragmentary, all these dimensions coexisted in the initial moments of stupor and curiosity about the event, without evolving beyond those rough outlines. None would achieve the solid footing or expansion of meanings that would appear later, when the theme of the grand political death ended up channeling all the news into coverage of collective mourning, displacing other dimensions of the case. Two or three weeks after the attack (the time it took to make the sea crossing from north to south), the illustrated magazines in the River Plate region began publishing images of the funeral in Rome: the monumental mortuary, the church where the ceremony took place, the motley procession of soldiers in the streets, the crowds that followed the cortege, and the burial itself. Appearing simultaneously in numerous cities, the images were a concise collection, and opened up the possibility of vicarious participation in memorial ceremonies for an important world event – at a distance.

In fact, the phenomenon had already begun. The arrival of the news via telegraph was followed by spontaneous gatherings in cities throughout the region. It soon became evident that it was not necessary to be in Monza, or Rome, or Italy, or in Europe at all to begin generating content about "the tragedy of Monza." The story broke away from its original setting, giving way to a range of local enactments. Occurring as it did in such a violent and surprising way, and at the height of the greatest expansion of Italian immigration in history, this death would provoke an outpouring of patriotic fervor in cities throughout the South American Atlantic. Countless ethnic associations mobilized public commemorations. In doing so, they demonstrated as never before the weight of their presence in those societies.

In the largest port cities, the phenomenon was massive. Crowds in the streets of Montevideo were accompanied by representatives of Italian organizations and political leaders. In Brazil, there were formal funeral ceremonies for King Umberto in Ouro Preto and Pará, though the largest took place in São Paulo. There, schools and businesses shut their doors and shrouded their facades in black crepe as columns of residents filed by. Immigrant associations brought in thousands more from interior towns.[66] Meanwhile, public demonstrations took place in neighborhoods all over Buenos Aires. Attended by the highest authorities, the official religious ceremony took place before an imposing catafalque in the

---

[65] *Caras y Caretas*, August 4, 1900.   [66] *Jornal do Brasil*, August 9, 1900, p. 2.

metropolitan cathedral. It continued in the street, with a full military parade and cavalcade of flower-laden coaches. Making its way through the streets, the procession arrived at a large grandstand engulfed by crowds. One foreign observer offered his take on the meaning of such a spectacle. "The magnificent scene," he said, spoke of "an immigrant community that feels like this is its own country."[67] As Martín Albornoz explains, the unprecedented scale of the demonstrations can be explained only by a confluence of three elements: the press's ability to generate a sense of synchrony with world events, a well-developed local culture of mobilization, and the strong patriotic impulse of the Italian community.

The movement would take on such a magnitude in the Argentine Pampas that *Caras y Caretas* prepared a special edition, an "Homage to Humberto I," compiling photographs from dozens of towns: one parade and memorial after another in the streets and squares of more than eighty municipalities, most of them located in the recently populated, fertile areas of the country.[68] A full month after the attack, the tragedy was giving rise to a phenomenon with its own momentum, one that repeated itself in public arenas, in a show of strength and vitality by the Italian community that compelled repeated expressions of solidarity on the part of long-standing local *criollo* elites.

Traces of this wave of demonstrations in 1900 can still be seen on any map of the Western South Atlantic region, underscoring the links connecting disparate points where Italian immigration was a decisive element, regardless of national boundaries. There are streets and avenues named "Humberto I" in Buenos Aires, São Paolo and Montevideo, of course; but also in Rosario, Mauá, Luján, Quilmes, Bahía Blanca and many others. There is a county named "Humberto I" in the Argentine Province of Santa Fe. Countless public buildings and monuments bear the name. Having become synonymous with Italian power in particular communities, that distant tragedy continued to leave its mark in the public space for many years. Mediated by municipal politics, it was the ultimate sign of the assimilation of global news into local agendas.

Showcases of Progress

On its cover of July 21, 1900, *Caras y Caretas* published a caricature of the mayor of Buenos Aires, Adolfo Bullrich. He was depicted balancing on the top of a tower near the port area. In one hand, he held an electric lamp, shining a beam of light into the darkness. "This is how the mayor/ hopes to receive the president/ whose arrival is expected/ next spring/ so that the reception/ will be more splendid," read the caption of the drawing (by the illustrator Mayol). The joke alluded to a much-talked-about matter in those days: the extravagant preparations for the visit of the Brazilian

---

[67] *La Prensa*, August 13, 1900, p. 3. [68] *Caras y Caretas*, September 20, 1901.

Image 2 *Caras y Caretas*, July 21, 1900

president Campos Salles, which included an unprecedented display of electric lights. Bullrich was made to look more like a set designer than a mayor. With cardboard tramways and rag flowers, his efforts resembled "set design applied to urban beautification." In one hand, the character holds a piece of paper that reads "For Campos Salles to see."[69]

---

[69] *Caras y Caretas*, July 21 and October 19, 1900. About these efforts: *La Prensa*, October 25, 1900, p. 5.

In the three months prior to the Brazilian president's arrival (the visit was between October 25 and November 1, 1900), the event's organization was an object of much attention in the Buenos Aires press. Although the visit was only a formal gesture of reciprocity (after the protocol visit of Argentine president Julio Roca to Rio de Janeiro the previous year), the city poured all its resources into the program. These events were part of a close-knit network of exchanges between such dignitaries, which over the course of the previous two decades had resulted in a remarkable political and cultural rapprochement.[70] As Ori Preuss has shown, figures linked to the Republican and anti-slavery cause, such as the abolitionist leader Joaquim Nabuco, were showing a growing interest in Buenos Aires; it was an expression of admiration on the part of the new Brazilian elites for changes the city had recently undergone. "It is no longer necessary to go to Paris," Nabuco said in 1889. "Everything that exists there can be found in Buenos Aires."[71]

It is worth pausing to examine this remark as it reveals the game of mirrors that governed these exchanges, and describes the place of Paris as an emblem of modernity, a status that hardly needs emphasizing. Of all the multiple meanings that Paris evoked among South American elites, none is stronger than its place as a global beacon of urban reform as embodied by Baron Haussmann in the 1860s. From then on, reform-minded mayors everywhere sought to follow this model, to produce their own more or less "Haussmannian" imprint in the dominant symbolic spectrum of progress.[72] Torcuato de Alvear, the first mayor of Buenos Aires after the federalization of the capital in 1880, had been inspired by Haussmann when he opened up the Avenida de Mayo, razing part of the oldest neighborhood in the town's colonial center in the process. In addition, a medical-hygienistic consensus (achieved after the epidemics of the 1860s and 1870s) led to a renovation of the sanitary system. Public buildings sprang up, and infrastructure vital to the project of opening to the world (mainly the port and railroads) was constructed.[73]

Campos Salles' visit took place at the moment when this modernizing ideology came to power in Brazil, together with the triumph of the Republic and the Paulista elites. The *entente* with Argentina's president Roca surprised no one, since both were promoters of projects that sought to integrate their respective countries into world markets. Moreover, in its early post-monarchy and post-slavery era, Brazil embraced an ambitious plan to attract European immigrants in an explicit attempt to "whiten" a society that had a large population of African descent.[74] Buenos Aires, with its bold urban reforms and immigration rates among the highest in the world, had become the inevitable point of reference.

---

[70] O. Preuss, *Transnational South America*, p. 77.   [71] Ibid., p. 73.
[72] Gorelik, *La grilla y el parque*, p. 101.   [73] Romero, "La ciudad burguesa."
[74] Skidmore, *Black into White*.

The story of this state visit is one of extravagant fraternal celebration. The scale of the preparations astounded local observers as the city prepared to make a spectacle of itself, to be seen and to make news. Returning to the caricature on the cover of *Caras y Caretas,* the message held by the mayor – "For Campos Salles to see" – might just as well have been directed at the Brazilian press, whose correspondents had arrived in droves and were welcomed with uncommon hospitality.[75] Most were well-known figures in a press network with a long history of mutual visits. In addition to prestigious writers and intellectuals, reporters of general information were able to participate in this exchange, facilitated as it was by the growth of maritime connections and the implementation of the underwater cable network between the two cities.

For a whole week, journalists from Rio would be taken around on guided tours, in which they could "discover" for themselves the clean streets, new facades lined with electric lights, booming construction and the health infrastructure. They would watch fire department maneuvers staged specially for them and visit cultural institutions and the headquarters of large newspapers. Between these tours, the contingent was treated to a rich itinerary of official entertainment, including banquets, palace dances, gala functions, carriage rides, flower displays, music, and mountains of gifts. For its part, the Buenos Aires press brought all of its resources to bear on the coverage of these festivities in extensive chronicles and special photographic supplements. After a few days, *Caras y Caretas* asked the visitors for their impressions. "Buenos Aires scares me," said the poet Álvares de Azevedo, a correspondent for *A Noticia*. "Its streets are a model: for their pavement, lighting, liveliness and stores whose windows display such variety. In short: I am stunned."[76]

Soon, this exhausting *tournée* would bear fruit in unanimously positive dispatches and articles in the newspapers of Rio de Janeiro. Buenos Aires was displaying "[t]rue wonders of luxury, the development of ideas, of arts and splendor," declared the *Jornal do Brasil*. Terse telegrams could not do justice to such brilliance, said the *Gazeta de Noticias*.[77] The envoy of *A Imprensa*, Arthur Dias, would publish a book with his own lavish praise of the city.[78] Bullrich's efforts had worked. Buenos Aires had been confirmed as "the capital of South America," and a massive press operation had extended this view to the thousands of readers who followed the coverage from Rio.

---

[75] Coelho de Souza Rodriguez, "Embaixadas originais"; *La Prensa*, October 25, 1900, p. 5.

[76] *Caras y Caretas*, October 27, 1900, p. 31.   [77] *Jornal do Brasil*, October 31, 1900, p. 2.

[78] Dias, *Do Rio a Buenos Aires, episódios e impressões d'uma viagem*; Baggio, "Dos trópicos au Prata."

The party ended, the contingent headed back, and soon the bright assessment gave way to a certain uneasiness. "With the mind stilled of this impression of a magical dream," said the poet Olavo Bilac (the main commentator for the *Gazeta de Noticias*), there began to arise "a profoundly sad conviction." "Any way you look at it, the Argentine Republic is much more advanced than Brazil." As memory settled, descriptions of the experience moved from expressions of fraternity, admiration and courtesy to comparison. The achievements of Buenos Aires were, in one way or another, Rio's failure. "All Brazilians are shocked by the sanitation and mortality figures," said one editorial. "[We] must clean and disinfect that open sore we call the Capital Federal, whose ostentatious rotten-ness, to foreign eyes, contaminates . . . the entire Republic of Brazil."[79] Even the clean-up in the aftermath of the festivities in Buenos Aires was judged to be superior: how quickly and efficiently the stages were dismantled, how the streets and parks were cleaned and restored to normal – so sanitary; so modern.

This superiority stood out even more in light of the disadvantages that Buenos Aires was seen to have overcome. Built upon the "crushing melancholy of an infinite plain" without shade or greenery, its environment was like "the muddy water of a meager river," Bilac observed. In contrast to this lack of charm, Rio was "nature's beloved daughter," located on a bay famous for its beauty, endowed with an undulating topography, bedecked in exuberant vegetation.[80] And this was precisely the problem: faced with a natural setting like "a dry and implacable stepmother," Buenos Aires had remained firmly on the path of progress, investing in hygiene and sanitation, its transportation system and its fire department. In a mere twenty years, it had surpassed Rio in all indicators of modernity. The only thing to do was to study and imitate this will to transform. Bilac said after his long, doleful comparison: "Don't be jealous, Rio de Janeiro."

The experience of the visit had confirmed, and expanded to many thousands, previous anecdotal perceptions about the transformation of Buenos Aires. Very soon, the spotlight turned inward. The uneasiness that marked this moment could be understood only in the context of a long cycle of debates around Rio's frustrated attempts at urban reform. In the 1880s, an ambitious renovation plan had been put in place, spearheaded by the engineer Francisco Pereira Passos, who had trained in Paris under the influence of Haussmann. Now, in a new political and ideological context, that project would be taken up again with renewed energy, and in much more radical terms than in Buenos Aires. In the years following that showcase visit, Rio would undergo its greatest transform-ation, entering a "*belle époque tropical.*" Old buildings and neighborhoods gave

---

[79] *Gazeta de Noticias*, November 5, 1900, p. 1; November 26, 1900, p. 1.

[80] *Gazeta de Noticias*, November 18, 1900, p. 1.

way to wide avenues, as priority was given to open air and light. Streets were paved, electric lights were installed. A strong French influence could be seen in the architecture of the many buildings under construction.[81] As has been shown in studies on the cycle of modernizing reforms in both port cities, each would adapt the Haussmann model to its own character and needs, refracting the Parisian model.[82]

The consolidation of Buenos Aires as a regional beacon of urban modernity would have repercussions of another kind, however, whose traces appear in a change in the tenor of the information exchanged between the two cities. To see how this took place, we must return to the end of the official visit, when the focus moved from fraternity toward competition to attract European immigrants.

It is a testimony to the disparate effects of the channels of communication that this change in tone did not come from the articles of the most distinguished representatives of Rio's cultural world (so well-received by their colleagues in Buenos Aires), but from satirical illustrations and regular telegraphic correspondence – a medium more prone to disruption and aggression. In the two previous decades, the emergence of a new information space had brought the daily life of the region's capitals closer together. In that heterogeneous system, readers in each city had a better sense of the other's contours than ever before – better even than those of many of their own country's towns that lay outside the major news circuits. But the nature of that new proximity did not quite match the kind of kinship imagined by the creators of the system (like Sarmiento), and there were many who saw in this new era of telegraphic language a dangerous tendency toward discord.[83]

Thus, in the months following the visit, cables transmitted from Buenos Aires to Rio show a shift in the selection of topics, with news of infectious diseases at the top of the agenda. There were many reports of outbreaks of smallpox, measles and tuberculosis in that city so recently lauded for its health infrastructure. Counterfeiters and criminals of all kinds were a problem, judging by the number of episodes mentioned in these dispatches. There were also many fires – it seems that the fire department was not so reliable after all. The same *Gazeta de Noticias* whose correspondents had been so eloquent on the relative advantages of Buenos Aires was now commenting on the micro-news on the cable with an unmistakable hostility. Editorials even speculated that these issues didn't make the news because the Argentine press was hiding them.[84] There was no reason

---

[81] Needell, *Belle époque tropical*, pp. 73–91.

[82] Gorelik, *La grilla y el parque*, pp. 101–102; Needell, *Belle époque tropical*, pp. 68–98.

[83] Britton, *Cables, Crises, and the Press*, pp. 328–333.

[84] The word *Porteño* will be used throughout this work to refer to the inhabitants of the port of Buenos Aires.

for potential immigrants to consider Buenos Aires more attractive than Rio unless they were swayed by a malicious editorial slant fostering the idea that tropical cities were less sanitary – a comment that provoked an imme-diate angry rebuttal by *La Prensa*.[85] Very soon, satirical illustration took charge of the spin. On page one of the *Gazeta de Noticias*, a pockmarked woman made a call to Milan from her Buenos Aires hospital bed: the "good air" of Buenos Aires was a lie, she warned her compatriots. So too were the rumors of an unhealthy climate in Brazil. In just a few months, admiration and fraternity had given way to a denunciation of "intrigues in the neighborhood."[86]

The illustrators of the Rio press began to portray their southern neighbor as a rich lady, dressed in the latest European fashion; a prosperous and somewhat vain figure, putting on airs of Frenchness. While initial representations might have shown her welcoming a visitor to the secrets of her triumph, later she was a deceiver, telling the poor, newly arrived European: "Don't go to my neighbor: he's dangerous."[87]

Less than a year had passed since those preparations that had embellished Buenos Aires for an occasion framed as a fraternal meeting. In fact, that display itself contained the seed of subsequent identity games, in which narratives of difference (in natural beauty, in modernity) shifted to languages less likely to be construed as friendly. Furthermore, the misleading agent portrayed in these cartoons was not "Buenos Aires" but "Argentina." It is a testimony to the role of the regional trans-urban network of news and connections that so many of the broader notions about the character of a neighboring country could be built upon images that were so specifically urban in their nature and selective in their scope.

In all cases, it was an asymmetrical game as Rio fixed its gaze on Buenos Aires more often than the reverse. We can recognize in that dynamic the traces of a more general configuration that was also apparent in the press of the region, in which the port city on the River Plate occupied a place that looked increas-ingly like a new kind of center, and functioned as an emblem for a whole nation. Whether in photographs or extended chronicles, or in the shorter and more trenchant language of the telegraph (and always accompanied by satirical illustrations), the press tended to crystalize these elements for the greater majority of readers. In this game of mirrors, there would be acknowledgments, contrasts and suspicion.

---

[85] *La Prensa*, April 27, 1901, p. 4. This summary stems from an overview of "Telegramas" from *Gazeta de Noticias*, April and May 1901.
[86] *Gazeta de Noticias*, April 27, 1901, p. 1.   [87] *Gazeta de Noticias*, April 21, 1901, p. 1.

Image 3 (a) Image 3 (b) *Jornal do Brasil*, November 1, 1900, p. 1; *Gazeta de Noticias*, April 21, 1901, p. 1

Remote Theaters of Imperial War

At the end of 1898, the poet and writer Rubén Darío was sent to Spain as a correspondent for *La Nación*. His close but critical vision of the state of things in Madrid began by noting the limited informative spectrum of peninsular newspapers: "They don't follow, as we do, the course of world events," he commented to his Buenos Aires readers.[88] Accustomed as they were to covering military conflicts in South America and Europe, newspapers in Buenos Aires were greatly expanding their "Exterior" sections with contents arriving from many other locations. Even today, those morning papers seem astonishing to the reader used to the more modest informative scope of the present Buenos Aires press.

In fact, the shift in the geographic spectrum of news had been a gradual process. For quite some time, the "News from Europe" arriving by steamship had concentrated on a cluster of countries: France, England, Spain and Italy, first of all, with some attention to Russia, Germany, Austria and Belgium. Such was the world as offered to readers in the 1860s and early 1870s. It was an

---

[88] Darío, *España contemporánea*, p. 30. Nicaraguan by origin, Darío had been living in Buenos Aires for five years and was a steady contributor to *La Nación* and other *Porteño* newspapers. Although his correspondence from Spain would cover a large selection of topics, his main mission was to report about the consequences of the country's terrible defeat by the United States in the war fought in Cuba in the previous months.

unsurprising selection, of course, given the convergence of long cultural traditions, demographic policies, and the reinforcement of an economic configuration focused on overseas trade. This is the context in which the new dispatches telegraphed by the Havas agency in 1876 were inserted, bringing the first signs of a destabilization of the picture. Indeed, the first news for this "South American service" went well beyond England, Spain or France, to focus on ongoing wars in the Ottoman Empire, followed by brief information on a number of other military and diplomatic conflicts in Eastern European territories.[89] To mitigate the bewildering effect this widening "Europe" may have had on readers, editors made sure to provide maps and additional background information about such regions. We have seen the parodies and jokes this first access to telegraphic news of the world provoked in the satirical press: they were a first glimpse of the effect the cable would have on spatial imagination.

With time, the scenario would extend much further, to include news of imperial wars in Asia and Africa. As the consolidation of cable technology led to more and more brief reports from the wider world, the reader in Buenos Aires would encounter an ever-growing host of city names in the morning paper: "Calcutta," "Cairo," "Hong Kong," "Bombay," "Teheran," "Tripoli," "Shanghai." Aside from the content of each piece, the format of the medium itself fostered the image of a constellation of cities all connected to each other, where the originating location was the first (and perhaps the only) thing that registered in a quick perusal of the news. It is not surprising, then, that the two *gauchos* parodied in *PBT* magazine – quoted in the opening of this Element – reflected on the evocative sounds of Russian city names, or that the mock "telegraph service" featured in the satirical weekly *Don Quixote* played with a cacophony of datelines from cities both local and foreign: Naples, Beijing, La Plata, Marseille, Montevideo, London.[90]

No matter how distracted the reader, no matter how ephemeral or dubious the content, the allocation of more column space, along with a layout in capital font emphasizing the names of distant cities, was not insignificant insofar as it represented in itself a transformation of an implicit world-horizon. This doesn't mean that a reader's understanding of geography was any less precarious, or that these names evoked "places" in the full sense of the word. It simply suggests that, at the most basic level, the proliferation of published telegrams brought with it a new repertoire of urban nomenclature. Such was the first expression of a change in the scale of the imagined world.

---

[89] *La Nación*, July 18, 1877, p. 1.   [90] *Don Quixote*, August 31, 1884, p. 3.

These names were distant and synchronous: "This is happening here"; "That is happening there." In this manner, dozens of brief items were displayed every day, written in a direct, standardized tone, as if not written by anyone. Aside from the relevance and readability of each unit, the pages containing international news – which were often subsumed in the section "Telegrams" – created the sense of a global quotidiàn, where the near and the far, the large and the small took their place in a world of urban points, all pulsating in unison.

The longer, more editorialized correspondence, dealing with the most important stories of the moment, was set against this diffuse background. The primacy of war news would lead wherever there were diplomatic tensions and battles to be reported, materials that the new information wholesalers (such as Havas and Reuters) offered to their remote customers as the most coveted material.[91] News of this kind was only exceptionally accompanied by images, as the access of photographers and correspondents to actual combat locations was limited by security considerations. As a result, most reporters were forced to combine briefings from the front with various forms of indirect coverage. This limitation explains the heightened focus on those cities associated with armed conflict – the larger urban centers, or even the smaller towns close to the action, where correspondents could access the telegraphic network connecting them to the global system. Thus, the Anglo-Boer War (1899–1902) would result in a wide circulation of visual coverage about Johannesburg and Cape Town, just as the Spanish-American War in Cuba (1898) brought to the forefront materials about Havana and Key West, a crucial telegraphic station during the episode.

The same would happen during the Boxer Rebellion of 1900, when that bloody confrontation between Chinese nationalists and European powers ushered in an unprecedented level of information about cities in that region. The exoticized distance with "the Chinese" was not confined to the South American press since that country and its culture had long been synonymous with "the distant" in a very extended Western subjectivity. Access to knowledge about that part of the world was indirect and tenuous, so the sudden flood of telegraphic deliveries found an audience who in all probability lacked a minimal set of interpretative guidelines.[92]

---

[91] Palmer, *Des petits journaux aux grandes agences,* pp. 103–138; Silberstein-Loeb, *The International Distribution of News*, pp. 163–174.

[92] Latin American "peripheral orientalism" has been the object of numerous critical analyses, mostly focused on the construction of the Islamic "other." See: Taboada, "Un orientalismo periférico." María Sonia Cristoff argues that the very lack of an interpretive tradition provided by

For those outside the narrow circles where travel literature about the "East" was available, that kind of knowledge was elusive indeed. As Rosario Hubert explains, access to Chinese literature in Buenos Aires would be shaped by the mediation of European languages, and by the fact that it tended to be available in bookstores rather than libraries, limiting its consumption to traditional critics and educated readers interested in foreign cultures.[93] Even among those who were familiar with this travel genre, context and points of reference were still lacking since it concentrated heavily on the cities of southern China, those with a strong English influence (such as Hong Kong), far removed from the area of the Boxer conflict. News would necessitate explanations about the status of cities in the north, such as Beijing and Tianjin, the port at the center of the international conflict, and home to many European delegations. "Tianjin is a city of great commercial and political importance, the administrative center of Chi-li province," said *Caras y Caretas*.[94]

Nor was there a readily available framework for political interpretations. The South American anti-imperialist discourse, then in its first developments, primarily focused on the United States' expansion – mainly in response to the recent Spanish-American War. The anarchist press maintained a critical view of the imperialist powers involved in the Boxer conflict, but this viewpoint set its sights on the evils of European expansion. Adopting the widespread depiction of the rebellion as "primitive," this vision of the conflict remained opaque and removed, rarely questioning in any serious way the reigning discourse pitting "civilization" against "barbarism."[95] With the rise of the left in the twentieth century, and the consolidation of the cultural influence of Communism in the 1930s and 1940s, more discriminating ways of understanding Chinese culture would arise, charged with fuller political meanings.[96]

A dearth of interpretive tools was not, however, an impediment to the flow of information about the Boxer Rebellion. For the most part, these news items were indirect, assembled by the South American correspondents based in London or Paris after passing through the mediation of the powerful European news agencies, either Havas or, more frequently, the *London Times* (and its correspondents in Shanghai). A typical column of

---

nineteenth-century travelers to the Far East explains the eclectic bent in the subsequent production of Argentine chronicles about this region. See: AAVV, *Pasaje a Oriente*, p. 15.

[93] Hubert, "Sinology on the Edge."   [94] *Caras y Caretas*, June 30, 1900.

[95] Bergel, *El Oriente desplazado*, p. 90.

[96] Bergel, *El Oriente desplazado*, pp. 125–173; Hubert, *Disorientations. Latin American Fictions of East Asia*, Chapter III, mimeo.

telegrams in *La Prensa* (the most widely read newspaper in Buenos Aires) juxtaposed four headlines on the morning of August 10, 1900: "Difficulties in Shanghai," "Details of the Battle of Peitsang," "More Killings in Chi-Li, " and "The Taking of Ying-Tsong."[97] This sort of briefing should not be taken as evidence of an active agenda in the public arena, however. The persistence of discrete informative units of this kind was also a strategy on the part of the modern newspaper to position itself in the market by including pieces that demonstrated its power and breadth of coverage. In fact, much of the telegraphic news of far-flung wars was included simply because it could be, beyond any particular relevance. No matter how many cables were printed, the limited echoes of the Boxer conflict stand in stark contrast with the immediate and resounding response to the anarchist attack on Umberto I.

In a weak interpretative context, the news of the Chinese conflict became a conduit for a patchwork of press materials, in which news about diplomacy and war was mixed with didactic cultural background and much cultural trivia. There was much to explain to readers in Buenos Aires. *Caras y Caretas* distilled the reporting on the diplomatic crisis into a display of tourist post-cards from the cities concerned. Thus, under the title "Events in China" there were photos of the "Porcelain Palace," the "Temple of Che-Fu," the "Ha-Ta-Men Gate in Beijing," the "Tomb of the Ming Emperors," the "Façade of the Ministry of Foreign Affairs in Beijing," "Main buildings of the Ming graves, a mausoleum and a temple," and a long list of landmarks.[98] China appeared as a collection of architectural wonders, ornaments, monuments and clothing; and the advance of the Boxers, not unlike the vandalization of an ancient museum.

Serene cities, remarkable structures, ancient sculptures, bustling markets and ports: once again, the genre of the photo-postcard sketched the con-tours of the remote city that now became the setting for major world events. Driven by the power of the news, these tropes reached far beyond their original circuit – individual use, the illustrated magazine, and the mail – and into the arena of mass media, where they were subjected to radical reconfigurations of meaning. Taking their place alongside portraits of politicians, soldiers and diplomats, these postcards of the monumental exoticism of the Chinese city were accompanied by epigraphs and explana-tory texts combining informative data with reports on the growing escal-ation of the conflict.

---

[97] *La Prensa*, August 10, 1900, p. 4.   [98] *Caras y Caretas*, July 14 1900.

LOS SUCESOS DE CHINA

achada del Tsung-Li-Yamen (Edificio del Ministerio de R. E. en Pekin)

Templo de la emperatriz en Wan-Shon-Sse

Image 4 *Caras y Caretas*, June 23, 1900

In the case of the most violent incidents (always attributed to the Boxers), the use of the building facade reappeared as a resource: "Pavilion of the imperial palace where the emperor is held hostage"; "Photo of the entrance to Tsu-Ling-Yamen, where the German minister was murdered"; "Residence of the Japanese delegation in Peking, set on fire by the boxers."[99] While leading readers on a path of learning about "the Chinese," the architectural postcard also fueled an idea of the distinct otherness of the forces threatening such monuments. Little or nothing was said, for example, about the looting of Chinese treasures by European troops.[100]

Limited as it was to the most basic and iconic composition of images – ancient temples and palaces, peaked ceilings – this coverage installed a particular repertoire of visual markers, which, despite reiteration, retained a large quotient of remoteness. The news sparked a wealth of humorous, trivial references to China, such as jokes based around the "ch" phoneme (say, in relation to Argentina's famously ubiquitous form of address, "Che"), or references to Chinese dress elements.[101] Outside of the incipient anti-imperialism of the libertarian press, the story offered little scope for developed opinion and conversation. In their extreme novelty and limited margin for appropriation, postcards of the Chinese city of 1900 might be seen as an echo of the telegraphic nomenclatures that filled the pages of newspapers. The frame of reception for

---

[99] *Caras y Caretas*, June 23 and June 30, 1900; July 14 and July 28, 1900.
[100] Hevia, "Looting and Its Discontents." [101] *Caras y Caretas*, July 28, 1900.

these fragments of news was improvised with many disparate tools, their superficial quality marking the conceptual limits of that much-expanded world horizon.

This imaginary stands in stark contrast to the density and weight of meaning attending other remote areas of the world and underscores the heterogeneous nature of the interpretative instruments that guided how information from afar unfolded in the newspapers of Buenos Aires. News of current events in Paris or Rome needed very little by way of clarification for it was received into a ready-made frame of reference brimming with significance and context. The Boxer War, on the other hand, gave rise to an endless series of piecemeal glosses, leaving much unexplained. Between these two extremes, other cases showed that incomplete notions about a distant city could be imbued with new meanings following the torrential pace of information.

Revolution in the Snowy City

News about the Russian Revolution of January and February 1905 arrived in the usual ways: correspondents in European capitals picking up information gleaned from the daily telegraph columns, and Havas including in the "South America" package whatever was sent by its correspondent in Saint Petersburg, with various forwarding combinations from different places adding more detail along the way. On the other side of the world, the first few inserts in the "Telegrams" column described a sequence of events, beginning with a workers' strike and leading to the atrocities of "Bloody Sunday" on January 22, when the czar's Cossacks massacred unarmed demonstrators in the streets of the city center. The events took place in an imposing setting, and the news was peppered with striking, resounding pieces of information: terrorist episodes attributed to anarchism, the participation of a well-known Orthodox priest (Pope Gapon), the imprisonment of the writer Maxim Gorky, among many others. At the end of February, *La Nación* sent one of its correspondents in Europe to Saint Petersburg to report directly on the social conditions there.

Distant in the extreme, this story immediately found its way into conversations in Buenos Aires. To begin with, everything about it resonated with the informational stream that for several years had brought scenes of protest and struggle in many European cities. Port workers, masons, miners, seamstresses: telegrams and images of workers taking to distant streets had become a news staple, a stable element in the daily picture of what happened in the world. All marked by concerns about the "social question" and the possibility of revolution, these reports provided a framework for thinking about more immediate expressions of unrest, which had intensified greatly in recent years.

The beginning of the century marked a culminating moment for workers' struggles in Buenos Aires, with strikes capable of shutting down ports and increased repressive violence in response. In 1902 the police established a "Social Order" division, dedicated to the surveillance of anarchists, the main force behind the protests and, by then, in control of the most powerful unions. That same year, a law was passed making it easier to expel foreigners, giving institutional form to the long accumulation of tensions around the pressing anarchist phenomenon, whose many manifestations were increasingly associated with the influence of "bad" immigration.[102] It was not difficult to reformulate the antinomies of distant Russia into more familiar terms. Whenever the "social question" and the dysfunction of the prevailing economic system came up as themes in the public arena, even the most distracted reader could draw a connection and conclude that local troubles were somehow related to those in other parts of the world.

Thus, the social dimension of the Russian conflict was easily translated into the local context. Naturally, it found its most direct counterpart in the libertarian press, where the connection between the two worlds was part of the very structure of the universe of references. In the newspaper *La Protesta*, which closely followed the unrest in European cities and often published doctrinal pieces on Russian anarchism, news about the uprising in Saint Petersburg appeared alongside the translated memoirs of Piotr Kropotkine. On the same page, one article called for a rally in support of the workers of that distant city: "no worker, no man of conscience should miss that important demonstration." The next day, the event was described as "a beautiful and eloquent demonstration of sympathy for the great Russian revolutionary movement."[103] Meanwhile, critics of abuse on the part of law enforcement adopted the term "Cossacks" to refer to the local city police. Class struggle joined in the synchrony that globalized news had set in motion.

In cosmopolitan Buenos Aires, one needn't have been a reader of leftist publications to know something about Russia. As we have seen, that

---

[102] Franco, "El estado de excepción a comienzos del siglo XX."
[103] *La Protesta*, February 2 and 3, 1905, p. 1.

country had long been part of the informational horizon of "Europe," albeit a somewhat occasional one, appearing mainly when its role in major questions of world politics came into play. Readers attentive to this aspect of the news were aware that the much-talked-about revolution was linked to the news of Japan's resounding victory in the Russo-Japanese war, which generated all sorts of speculation about the rise of that nation and the decline of Russia.[104]

Meanwhile, the latest news activated visions of the world of power in those lands, sparking many fantasies. Images of the czars' residence appeared occasionally in illustrated revues and magazines, since the worldly life of the Romanoffs was part of the coverage of the social life of European aristocracies, which held a certain voyeuristic appeal in societies with rather austere republican institutions. In the popular magazine *PBT*, "Pictures from the Czar's Bedroom" could function just as well in the context of political reportage as in a section of miscellaneous curiosities "From Everywhere," suggesting a certain exoticization of the extravagance of this remote elite.[105] Playing on the overwhelming geographic and social distances, one humorous piece imagined a letter to the czar sent by a simple *Porteño* from a corner mailbox in Buenos Aires. Written in colloquial *criollo* rhyme, it addressed the legendary monarch in a plebeian tone, advising him to provide education for the people and to renounce the "haughty pride" that had caused so much bloodshed.[106]

The sheer enormity of political differences could be used to shed light on the local situation. The "Russian drama" was a "clash of epochs" between "the monarchical ideal of the past and the democratic ideal of the present," explained *Caras y Caretas*.[107]

All of these appropriations, of course, combined the recent news from Russia with visions derived from that powerful engine of imagery, popular literature. Thanks to readily available translations in cheap editions, many readers were able to draw connections between the current events and what they had gleaned from the fictional universes of Tolstoy, who was widely

---

[104] As M. Bergel shows, the Russo-Japanese War was extensively covered in Buenos Aires, including through a vast array of images of the decisive Port Arthur battle. "En el país de los crisantemos. Enrique Gómez Carrillo y las derivas de la guerra ruso-japonesa en la prensa porteña", *Prismas. Revista de historia intelectual*, 25 (2021), pp. 199–208.

[105] *La Ilustración Española y Americana*, October 30, 1894, p. 5; *PBT*, March 4, 1905, p. 21.

[106] *PBT*, February 4, 1905, p. 31; March 4, 1905, p. 5; *Caras y Caretas*, February 25 and March 4, 1905.

[107] *Caras y Caretas*, March 4, 1905.

read and admired. His reputation went beyond the realm of narrative as he was regarded as a kind of sage who embodied all at once Christianity, pacifism, vegetarianism and anarchism.[108] Also gaining prominence in those days were the ideas of the poet and writer Gorky, whose imprisonment at the hands of czarist forces was widely reported. One particular photo picturing him walking the snowy streets under the watchful eyes of his jailers would find its way from European illustrated magazines to *Caras y Caretas*. As an icon of the resistance, Gorky also earned himself a detailed, though not uncritical profile in *La Nación*, the most literary of Buenos Aires' newspapers.[109]

Tolstoy and Gorky could well move from the prestigious cultural supplement to pieces dealing in more commonplace commentary. These two famous writers came up in the chat "between *gauchos*" that we began with. As they drank their *mate*, these characters also discussed the social problems in that distant land. The names of "those writers of high ideas" were subject to a slapstick of *criollo* phonetics: Maxim Gorky became "Máximo Gazques," Tolstoy was "Tuesta hoy" (toast today) and Dostoyevsky was mutilated into "De esto es yesca" (Of this is tinder). Better to learn to pronounce the Slavic names, concluded one of the *gauchos*: soon the great dukes themselves would be emigrating "as this place is a refuge for all kinds of foreigners who are in trouble."[110]

This revolution arrived accompanied by distinctive names and cityscapes. The event was inextricably linked to Saint Petersburg, and its narration made good use of the singular character of the place. The most dramatic incidents were centered in the heart of the czars' city, in its famous streets and in the shadows of its iconic buildings. As was common in the coverage of distant episodes, photo-postcards set the stage, gradually establishing the scene of the news. To help with location references, coverage of "Bloody Sunday" included a map of Saint Petersburg. This was no generic map, merely pinpointing the location of an episode. Rather, these were detailed diagrams showing the city's great landmarks, and where they lay in relation to the massacre. Like Baedeker's reference list, *La Nación* offered tools to understand the location of buildings and monuments: bridges over the Neva, the Winter Palace, the Nevsky

---

[108] Albornoz, "O reino de Deus entre nós?"
[109] *La Nación*, March 5, 1905; *Caras y Caretas*, March 11, 1905.
[110] *PBT*, February 4, 1905, p. 32.

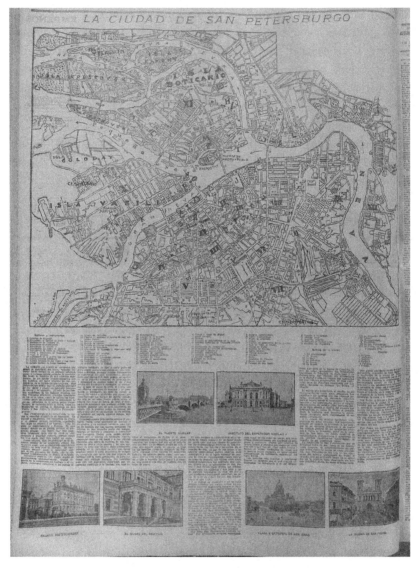

Image 5 *La Nación*, January 26, 1905

Prospect, the Hermitage, Saint Peter's Church, and then more postcards of
more palaces and more bridges. Continuing the didactic approach to
reporting on remote regions, these events became an occasion to introduce
readers to the history of the elegant Nevsky Prospect, accompanied by
a photo taken months before, like a souvenir from a guided tour.

This eye-catching visual device was juxtaposed with a narration of the atrocities taking place there. Built on the back of the people's misery, the majestic capital seemed like the cradle of imminent catastrophe. *La Nación* wrote: "Beneath the lively appearance of its streets, Saint Petersburg hides a painful shadow of fear and oppression."[111] *La Ilustración Española y Americana*, on the other hand, condensed both aspects into a single map. Right beside the recent horrors – the city's dark side – the main features of Peter the Great's capital were explained and its most dazzling features described.[112]

Russia had a long tradition of illustrated photographic postcards. In wide circulation, they included abundant propaganda from the czarist empire. In the months prior to the conflict, the revolutionary opposition began disseminating its own publicity via the medium. The leaders of the uprising were keenly aware of the power of the image, and maintained tight control over what correspondents were permitted to photograph. In the aftermath of "Bloody Sunday," images of confrontations between Cossacks and civilians were sent all over Europe, with high levels of circulation within émigré communities. These images would soon become iconic.[113] While it is impossible to establish the ultimate origin of the selections that reached the South American press, it is clear that European magazines played an important part in mediating this access. They in turn were dependent on a variety of sources connected directly with correspondents and revolutionaries on the scene. By the end of February, readers in Buenos Aires could appreciate how the latent tension of those prior images – of those silent buildings, the city-as-museum – suddenly erupted into a multitude of dramatic, sometimes violent street scenes in a confrontation of epic proportions.[114]

The dramatic intensification of these latest scenes was accompanied by a loss of visual quality not only due to the nature of the photos themselves (action shots rather than static images) but also because of the multiple reproductions needed to cross such distances in a hurry. For the sake of narrative clarity, the images were subjected to some rather conspicuous touching-up. Thus, this later collection occupied an intermediate zone between photograph and illustration, underscoring the contrast with the earlier postcards of monumental Saint

---

[111] *La Nación*, January 26, 1905, p. 4; the story about the Nevsky Prospect appeared January 25, p. 4.

[112] *La Ilustración Española y Americana*, February 8, 1905, p. 72.

[113] Rowley, *Open Letters*, ch. 7.

[114] *PBT*, March 4, 1905, p. 5; *Caras y Caretas*, February 25 and March 4, 1905.

Image 6 *PBT*, March 4, 1905

Petersburg. The enhancements had the effect of imbuing the scenes with a certain schematic urgency.

The extreme cold – evident in the snow that blanketed everything, in the clothing people wore, and in the many sleds in the streets – added to the drama of the scenes. An important element in the public imagination of faraway Russia, the cold had a place in the conversation about events occurring "over there." In an imagined meeting with the Russian czar, a "PBT boy" (dressed in boots and a fur coat) explained to readers: "[T]here the cold is so severe you have to put your hands in molten steel to avoid freezing to the bone."[115]

The hemispheric inversion of the seasons was an implicit fact of the "foreign" news offering, and an element that could put into relief like few others the contextual contrasts born of informational synchrony. Snow (whether in Russia, Germany or the United States) produced wonder, amazement, recognition and a touch of the uncanny. Though originally intended for local consumption in its

INFORMACIÓN EXTRANJERA

EL MOVIMIENTO REVOLUCIONARIO EN RUSIA

Tropas acampadas en las calles de San Petersburgo

El funeral de una víctima de la gran carga en las calles de San Petersburgo

Image 7 *PBT*, March 11, 1905, p. 5

---

[115] *PBT*, February 25, 1905, p. 30.

cities of origin, news about the problems posed to urban infrastructure by the boreal winter became part of a much wider circuit, where it took on other meanings. At the end of that journey, the inconveniences of blocked streets and burst pipes became a mere curiosity, yet another phenomenon of the variegated world. Without direct experience of its destructive power, snow was seen as adornment, an abstract and unattainable accessory, otherworldly and marking a line between "here" and "there."

Not only did it never snow in the capitals of the American South Atlantic, but the news from Russia arrived during high summer, mixing with advice on how to protect oneself from the sun and postings from seaside vacation spots. Photos of the Revolution coincided with the eve of Carnaval, inspiring some to dress up as the czar or Pope Gapon.[116] In tropical Rio de Janeiro, the *Jornal do Brasil* described events in Russia in words that pointed to this exotic contrast: "White snow and red blood! Religious chants and bugle calls!"[117] Meanwhile, the cover drawing of Rio's *Revista da Semana* featured an image of the czar confronting his people from a balcony. The snow-covered letters of the name of the magazine made the context instantly identifiable.

Snow was a recurring theme in the chronicles of the Guatemalan correspondent Enrique Gómez Carrillo, who traveled from Paris to Saint Petersburg to report for Madrid's *El Imparcial* and Buenos Aires' *La Nación*.[118] Working against clichés so prevalent in warm countries, this chronicler emphasized the realities of extreme winter conditions, underscoring the value of his own direct (in situ) experience in the process. "You who have not been here have no idea what this word means. Snow is the terrible divinity, the enduring obsession." He wanted to explain not only snow to his readers but also the cold, and the strangeness of winter sun; a pale and formless presence: "like a gnawed and battered monstrance seen through opaque lenses." Gómez Carrillo would go on to produce a vast journalistic report with abundant data on the social conflict. Along the way, his interest in revising the commonplaces attached to the Russian landscape would filter through, resulting in a vision that was both more imposing and more contradictory: "The snow! The snow! How beautiful, but how cruel!"[119]

An experienced and talented travel writer, Gómez Carrillo used his skills to bring Saint Petersburg's cold and snow to his readers in the Southern hemisphere. In that city of domes, where "everything is grand in the panorama," and where "the streets have no end and disappear into the horizon," he found the

---

[116] *PBT*, March 4, 1904, p. 28.   [117] *Jornal do Brasil*, January 26, 1905, p. 1.

[118] Gómez Carrillo, *La Rusia actual*. On the oriental travels of Gómez Carrillo, and his visit to Saint Petersburg: Siskind, *Cosmopolitan Desires*, pp. 223–259.

[119] Gómez Carrillo, *La Rusia actual*, p. 186.

Image 8 *Revista da Semana*, February 5, 1905

(similarly grand) Neva River completely frozen, scattered with icebound ships, and solid enough for wagons to cross. Under its bridges, street vendors would warm their samovars. "The eyes never get tired of contemplating it. It is the most singular, the most exotic thing that a southern imagination can picture," he said, mindful of his readers' distance and their lack of experience of severe winter.[120]

---

[120] Ibid., p. 187.

Very soon, however, the dazzling white of Saint Petersburg gave way to a thaw, revealing the hidden city beneath the "enamel." The correspondent couldn't hide his disappointment. Deprived of the cloth that gathered their spaces together and covered their defects, the immense and the sumptuous were exposed in all their exaggeration and folly. As Gómez Carrillo saw it, in the course of one night, Saint Petersburg had left Europe and gone to Asia, from civilization to barbarism, rousing in him the most merciless of orientalist reflections. Suddenly an improvised, inharmonious city was revealed – "something like a World's Fair district." Even the famous Nevsky Prospect looked clumsy and graceless, ostentatious and naive with its overly adorned windows. Perhaps it was the effect of the thaw, he conceded. "Maybe everything here is meant to be seen in the snow. Every city needs its own particular mood, its own sky, its own sun. And today the flakes have not fallen, and the king of the Arctic has not blown above us. It is as if in Seville the sun were not to rise one day."[121]

The Catastrophe City

In late 1899, an illustrator for *Caras y Caretas* offered a typology of the consumers of that successful magazine. It did not include women, though there were many among its readers. It portrayed instead a motley group of typical urban male characters: the follower of high society gossip, the puzzle fanatic, the reader of humorous articles, two immigrants dressed as Mediterranean peasants, absorbed in the international news. Finally, the group included a man leaning forward in his chair, with an expression of rapt alarm on his face: the reader of "crimes, revolutions and catastrophes."

It might not be apparent from looking at these characterizations, but the content that so attracted and shocked this reader was by and large "international" as well. Much of the news coming out of the global network replicated the taste for sensationalism cultivated in publications all over the world. And, as in other press markets, a considerable part of this offering stemmed from everyday occurrences – crime, accidents, fires, etc.[122] The spectacularization of the city in the 1900s owes much to this tendency. So widespread was this development, and so eloquent its effects, that it has inspired an important line of analysis of the turn-of-the-century press, a perspective that focuses on the newspaper's role in the sensory ("neurological") experience of the modern

---

[121] Ibid., p. 197.

[122] Singer, "Modernity, Hyperstimulus, and the Rise of Popular Sensationalism," pp. 72–99; Kalifa, *L'encre et le sang*; Caimari, *Apenas un delincuente. Crimen, castigo y cultura en la Argentina moderna* (Buenos Aires: Siglo XXI, 2004), pp. 165–247.

El de los crímenes, revoluciones y catástrofes

Image 9 *Caras y Caretas*, October 7, 1899

city, and in its capacity to exacerbate the commotion with its aesthetics of astonishment, in confusing and fragmented scenarios.[123]

Reporting about urban violence was an essential aspect of a press that proved its modernity by taking reporters out of the newsroom and putting them on the streets all over the world. It was a modern, and also eminently local approach, since talking about problems of the city meant, first of all, talking to one's own city. It was precisely this local character that made so much of this news irrelevant to the South American correspondent in search of content for his distant readers. First to be discarded were stories that presupposed a familiarity with the quarrels and antagonisms of municipal governments or recognition of specific nuances of identity – ethnic and neighborhood contrasts, differences between center and suburb, rivalries between cities of a region. Also outside the spectrum were pieces dealing with failures of infrastructure, or the state of particular reformist agendas. None of this survived the long-distance journey: the effectiveness of this sort of content dissolved as soon as it crossed a certain threshold, no farther than a few kilometers.

Other kinds of subject matter, however, effortlessly found their place in the global circuit, becoming permanent items on the information agenda. A powerful point of intersection would be consolidated between the new

---

[123] This perspective has a crucial point of inspiration in Georg Simmel's seminal essay on the effects of urban life (Berlin was his case) on the modern psyche; see Simmel, "The Metropolis and Mental Life."

Image 10 *PBT*, February 11, 1905, p. 21

urban journalism and the demands of a system in which certain local content was nevertheless pertinent to consumers with no connection to the original context. Even if municipal policy was not easily exportable, stories of accidents, landslides, fires and floods showed themselves to be quite adaptable to the language of mainstream news. Sensational on its face, the disaster story demanded little decoding effort and did not need the kind of follow-up provided by a stable community of readers required by political stories. News of calamity and disaster generated immediate astonishment and interest; it was well suited to the medium of the telegraph and lent itself to understandable, eye-catching photographic images. It is not surprising that the "packages" transmitted by correspondents and agencies were keen on including such material. The "Telegrams" sections of the great newspapers of Buenos Aires rarely let a day go by without some news of a fire, a collapsed building, or an earthquake.

Very little in the way of content participated more clearly in the logic of the turn-of-the-century spectacle, connecting news with other circuits of cultural consumption. It is worth recalling the intense interest in "attractions" films in many Latin American cities, where itinerate companies showed compilations of short news footage from around the world.[124] Emblematic magazines of the era, such as *Caras y Caretas* and *PBT*, cultivated an analogous genre in their (very successful) regular sections: "From all over the world," "The rare and curious," "From everywhere," all made up of selections of globally circulating materials. The logos themselves alluded to the operation of cartographic assembly and disassembly implicit in these constructions.

The world was a storehouse of rarities, of the unusual, the extreme and the exceptional. The modern reader was exposed to a juxtaposition (a collage, in Anthony Giddens' words) of more particles than before; more flashes of events detached from experience.[125] On the pages of these sections, a strange building in Scotland could coexist with confetti-making in Italy, Siamese twins in

---

[124] López, "Early Cinema and Modernity in Latin America."

[125] In his work on the advent of modern identity, Anthony Giddens refers to the *collage effect* of the late nineteenth-century press, transformed by commercial criteria and information technology; see Giddens, *The Consequences of Modernity*, p. 27.

Turkey, a clay village in Lower Egypt, a child prodigy who could play the piano at the age of three, a museum where a banquet was held beneath the skeleton of a brontosaurus, a Burmese hearse, an embalmed dog in San Luis, or a peach tree with the face of an owl. This last discovery, captured by a local photographer, "deserves to go around the world, to be reprinted by foreign colleagues, and most likely it will, since so many people are hunting for this kind of novelty," commented *PBT*.[126] The desired access to the "world" also included sharing in a range of curiosities and astounding discoveries.

There had always been a place in the South American press for news of great urban disasters. This was well represented in the first illustrated magazines of the 1860s and 1870s, when the link between image and journalism was in its early stages. But the expansion of sensational news as enticing content and the emergence of photography in newspapers and magazines would cement its place in the "world news" of the turn of the century. Artistic illustrations held their own in this process as a narrative complement to what the photographer had not been able to capture: the exact moment of the collapse, the train derailment, victims of a fire pleading for rescue from the windows of the building. But the "truth" of the photograph – even the half-truth of the blatantly retouched photograph – would gain ground in the coverage.

Caras y Caretas featured several scenes of disaster in each issue. They were gathered from its various sources: its own photographers, stringers from the provinces, spontaneous witnesses to an event, from a cliché acquired from a foreign magazine, or reproductions of imported prints. Everything converged to feed the sequence of the week: "The storm in Valparaiso"; "Fire in a convent in Segovia"; "Derailment of an electric tramway"; "The fire in the Comedy Theater in Paris"; "Hail stones in Madrid"; "Floods in the province"; "The hurricane in Texas"; etc. As the magazine itself explained, these photographs were follow-ups to cables that had arrived earlier, closing the gap between the instantaneity of that medium and the slower physical journey of the visual document. The news was known. The subsequent arrival of the images completed (and intensified) that news.

With its brief, explosive intrusion, catastrophe had the power to destabilize the world horizon constructed by other pieces of information. Geographic hierarchies were still there, of course. The great fire of the Charité at Rue Goujon, in Paris, garnered more coverage and commanded more market value than would a similar event in any other city, making its way into the morning routines of innumerable readers, far and wide.[127] The same principle held true

---

[126] *PBT*, April 1, 1905, p. 24.

[127] The great fire of the Parisian Bazar de la Charité (May 4, 1897) killed 130 people, including members of the aristocracy.

for any local disaster: a fire in Buenos Aires (where reporters for the country's main media were, and still are, located) attracted more attention than a fire in a provincial city. However, the "news value" of a city could be raised abruptly by a major disaster, altering the usual habits of attention. This happened from time to time in connection with earthquakes in the Andean region. These forced the press to look westward from the Atlantic coast, bringing into view communities and populations that had been largely absent from the usual news agenda.

Earthquakes happened in many parts of the world, of course, and the telegraphic columns reported on them with remarkable diligence.[128] The informative relevance of the event was directly proportional to the scale of the destruction and the number of victims, so the earthquakes most attended to were, by far, those that affected large cities. This is why it was so important to secure the precision of the first pieces of information as they passed through multiple stages of retransmission. The news of an earthquake in Panama, for example, was cabled by Havas-Paris to Pernambuco (Brazil) with a clarification that there were no victims ("nulle victimes"). However, upon arrival the information was transcribed as "mille" (one thousand), and then redistributed to the entire South American network. Several operators were reprimanded: some for absentmindedness, others for using words that lent themselves to confusion. The error had resulted in the item being misplaced in the all-important hierarchy of news priorities.[129]

When a great earthquake struck the Chilean port city of Valparaiso, on August 16, 1906, it wasn't the first time the press faced the challenge of covering an event of this kind. Twelve years earlier, in 1894, readers had learned of the widespread destruction in two cities in northwestern Argentina: La Rioja and San Juan. The same selective criteria that brought Paris, Rio de Janeiro or Saint Petersburg into the news feed had then yielded a host of images of these two cities. They were not so distant, of course: these were provincial capitals within Argentina's national territory. But they lay outside the main avenues of Atlantic-centered news circulation. Now, as a result of a natural disaster, news of these two traditional Andean towns found its way onto the front page of morning papers. Organized around a narrative of "before and after," postcard images of churches, public buildings and old houses were juxtaposed with illustrations (by artists hired by *La Nación* and *La Prensa*) of what those buildings had now been reduced to.[130] *La Ilustración Sud-Americana*, on the

---

[128] On the telegraphic report of earthquakes in the early twentieth century: Winder, "Telecommunications Technology and News of Disaster."

[129] Letter from Havas to Baccani, November 10, 1882, Archives Nationales de France, Fonds Havas, 37 1, p. 109.

[130] *La Nación*, November 16, 1894; *La Prensa*, November 5, 1894. Martín Malharro was the artist in the first case, José Stalleng in the second. On the long-lasting effects of earthquakes in San Juan, and its development pattern, see: Healey, *The Ruins of the New Argentina*.

VISTA PANORAMICA DE SAN JUAN

Image 11 (a and b) "San Juan Earthquake," *La Ilustración Sud-Americana*, November 20, 1894, pp. 512 and 516, respectively

other hand, combined a serene daytime postcard of San Juan with a narrative image dramatizing the terror and panic of the inhabitants as the event occurred by artist and founder of the magazine Rafael. J. Contell.

More than a decade had passed when news of the disaster in Chile reached the Atlantic coast. In the intervening years, a reliable postal route had been established among the main cities of Chile, Argentina and Uruguay, thanks to the railroad that linked the Valparaíso/Santiago axis with the ports of Buenos Aires and Montevideo. It had succeeded in reducing delivery times from several weeks to just three or four days and had led to a remarkable increase in the volume of correspondence and printed matter.[131] In combination with the Trans-Andean telegraph line, the system guaranteed an efficient correspondence service between ports on both shores. Yet, just as the global communication network had diminished the relative visibility of Argentina's interior in the newspapers of Buenos Aires, it had also brought closer together those ports and cities that were well-connected to the system (a product of the same logic we have seen in the case of Buenos Aires and Rio de Janeiro). Indeed, on the regional level, the configuration of this informative space was more distinctively trans-urban than transnational – as it is more usually described when

---

[131] Caimari, "La carta y el paquete."

REPUBLICA ARGENTINA – PROVINCIA DE SAN JUAN – UNA ESCENA DEL TERREMOTO
(Dibujo de R. J. Corrall.)

Image 11 (a and b) Cont.

analyzing specific networks – transforming information flows and reducing subjective distances among a number of cities rather than entire nations.

The earthquake, estimated to have registered a massive 8.2 on the Richter scale, brought a sudden and severe interruption to this circulation system. For several days, information coming out of Valparaiso depended on a messenger who rode on horseback to the nearest telegraph office, and on whatever information was transmitted via telegraph among the postmasters of neighboring countries.[132] It is worth looking more closely at the further development of this story in the Buenos Aires press, and the sudden focus on Valparaiso.

---

[132] *La Nación*, August 19, 1906, p. 7; Martland, "Reconstructing the City, Constructing the State," 236.

So uncertain was the information at the beginning of the news cycle that it was not even clear which cities were affected. The disaster was still very much an imprecise and choppy account of death and destruction when newspapers and magazines began publishing postcards of Chilean urban centers, drawing on available images from self-celebratory collections of progress and modernity. Photo-postcards of this kind were not unknown or unusual. They had been circulating in illustrated magazines for some time. Weeklies such as *La Ilustración Sud-Americana* and *La Ilustración Española y Americana* routinely covered official visits, national holidays and anniversaries, including photographs of Argentine, Uruguayan and Chilean cities. In the news- oriented *Caras y Caretas*, images of other disasters (a fire, a particularly destructive storm in Valparaiso or Santiago) were occasionally deployed. There was also a place for high society events – an elite marriage, a sumptuous funeral, etc. Such was the kind of low-degree presence of Pacific-coast cities in the Buenos Aires illustrated press.

The damage to the communication routes produced an additional delay in the availability of images, which further strained the relationship between breaking news and journalistic photography. The "before" images, which were beginning to hone in on Valparaiso, coexisted with a jumbled sequence of alarming telegrams, whose information was of uncertain veracity. They alluded to thousands of dead, absolute destruction and general panic, even as increasingly anachronistic images of visual landmarks of the city in question continued to circulate (the panorama of the bay, the squares and public buildings, docks, some national monuments, the elegant avenues of La Victoria and Prat, the Costanera Errázuriz, even the interiors of great mansions). They depicted a modern, orderly city; a port designed and built in the "European style" thanks to strong commercial links – evidence of the cosmopolitan agenda of its leaders – and reforms carried out by its municipal authorities.[133] Presented under headlines that spoke of catastrophe, these postcards of urban progress became views of the city "on the verge of being destroyed," "the city unaware of its fate," thus casting an ominous shadow over photos originally conceived of as an optimistic promotion of order and progress.[134]

It would take three weeks for images of the disaster to reach newsrooms, where special supplements were put together, completing the operation. Since the earthquake in La Rioja and San Juan, journalism had been transformed by

---

[133] *La Ilustración Española y Americana*, August 30, 1906, p. 125 ff.; *Caras y Caretas*, August 25, 1906, p. 43 ff.; *La Nación*, August 19, 1906, p. 6. On the modernization of Valparaíso: Martland, *Construir Valparaíso*, pp. 101–194.

[134] On this photographic genre: Tell, *El lado visible*, pp. 99–156.

Image 12 *La Nación*, August 19, 1906, p. 6

photography. These new images were sharp, reinforcing the sense of proximity to the drama.

There was little to add to the devastating power of these scenes of streets lined with mangled buildings, homes destroyed, makeshift shelters and a cemetery in disarray. Unlike the previous images, which had provided explanations with their presentations of the city-scene, these photos were accompanied by

Image 13 *La Nación*, September 8, 1906

minimal captions, sometimes just the name of the street or building in question. Some showed human figures: men, women and children amid the desolate panorama, a victim waiting for an ambulance, refugees from a camp staring into the camera, uniformed authorities giving instructions. These figures added narrative meaning (material and emotional) to the terrible destruction that dominated the frame: a theater reduced to rubble, "what's left of La Merced," "one of the finest buildings on the avenue," "Don Jorge Montt's house, where his wife and daughter were crushed."[135]

The earthquake had ravaged the wealthiest and most prominent sections of Valparaiso, especially the large neighborhood of Almendral, which was built on land gained from the sea when the port was expanded. There, government buildings, commercial and social centers, and exclusive neighborhoods were hit hardest. Since they tended to be the same areas that had been featured in those postcards a few days earlier, these images of destruction completed the symmetry of "before and after." "It is said that not a single important building has been spared," said *La Nación*, "and that among those destroyed by fire are the arsenals, the naval academy, the customs office, the maritime governor's office, the Royal Hotel, Mrs. Ross Edwards' palace, and the *El Mercurio* newspaper." The effects of the disaster on poorer areas, those on the mountain, were barely mentioned.[136]

As dramatic images and reports gained momentum, the interpretation of the disaster was shedding some of the meanings it acquired in its original setting. Little was said in the Atlantic press, for example, about confrontations between citizens and troops belonging to the Chilean central government, or about the abuses of martial law reported by inhabitants of the port. As Samuel Martland shows, the initial reaction of the authorities was decidedly repressive, addressing the situation in terms of the danger of disorder and crime. Such episodes began a long cycle of intervention by the national government in municipal matters in Valparaiso, supplanting local authorities in the process of reconstruction that lay ahead.[137] This crucial development had local and national significance, and would be largely ignored in the transnational (trans-urban) coverage.

One other important aspect of the event evaporated on its way east: the voyeuristic spectacle of suffering and destruction lost the pedagogic value it held at its point of origin, and anywhere else where earthquakes occurred. In Buenos Aires, where seismic activity was non-existent and fear of earthquakes was unknown, that component of the news simply did not translate, say, into reflecting about approaches to building construction. This splitting off of one aspect of the news due to geographical conditions where it was received can be contrasted with other points of resonance with urban catastrophe at the time, such as fire.

---

[135] *PBT*, September 15, 1906, pp. 11–39; *Caras y Caretas*, September 8, 1906; *La Ilustración Española y Americana*, October 8, 1906, p. 204.

[136] On the areas of Valparaiso destroyed during the earthquake: Martland, *Construir Valparaiso*, p. 199.

[137] Martland, "Reconstructing the City, Constructing the State," 222–252; Martland, *Construir Valparaíso*, p. 199.

At the end of the nineteenth century, fires were well established in the information agenda of industrial cities. The theme had a long genealogy, extending back before the modernization of the press. Though fire had always been a danger, and controlling it was a perennial struggle for the human species, the industrial era had brought new danger with its use of fossil fuels in factories. "It no longer affected fields, farms, forests, and wilderness, but cities, manufacturing, commerce, capitalism, politics, technology, and social order," explains Stephen Pyne. This increased danger of fire in urban environments would bring with it new conceptions of the role of human societies in controlling it.[138] As we have seen, the proliferation of accidents in factories and working-class housing was widely covered in the press, giving greater visibility not only to narratives of tragedy and loss but also to prevention.

Few news stories combined so explicitly the spectacular with the pedagogical. Captured by photojournalists in cities large and small around the world, fire produced a relatable story, effortlessly adaptable to practically relevant frameworks of local meaning. The South American press made great use of this theme. Its trail can be seen in all forms of news – from the telegram to the narrative correspondent, from illustration to photography. This interest was not only due to the marketability of the event, or its brief sensory (and commercial) impact. The statistics regarding fire departments (at that time in different stages of professionalization) clearly reflected the incidence of this threat in the life of the region's cities.[139] Reports on overcrowding and poor conditions in collective housing were common topics in municipal policy debates, where the influence of hygienism and urban planning ideologies held sway over modernization plans. It is worth remembering that consumers of these stories were largely concentrated in port cities where immigration was driving the rapid construction of housing, in structures that were often precarious and inadequate. The dangers they posed were at the center of discussions about the "social question."

While news of fire involving factories or low-income housing was the most common, theater fires were the most sensational, and they had multiplied. An important institution at the core of turn-of-the-century cultural life (in Rio as well as Buenos Aires and Montevideo), theaters provided venues for local drama associations and regional troupes and were obligatory stops for opera companies on the Atlantic circuit. In this context, news about a terrible theater fire in a European city contained a pedagogical component. In her study of the

---

[138] Pyne, *Fire*, p. 155.

[139] De Souza, "Heróis das Chamas"; on this development in the context of the modernization of Mexico City, see Alexander, *City on Fire*, pp. 5–11; on fire services in Valparaíso, see Martland, *Construir Valparaíso*, pp. 49–72.

coverage of these incidents in Buenos Aires, Kristen McCleary draws attention to the preventive function these stories served.[140]

Unlike this easily relatable archive of disasters, the spectacle of the terrible earthquake in Valparaiso seemed to lose more meanings than it gained on its journey from one city to another. And yet, a glance at the informative context of arrival illuminates what was also added in the journey. Rather than providing eventual lessons for city planners and municipal authorities, the same images that generated horror and empathy underscored the profound differences in the kinds of urban problem the two port cities faced. If the news turned its gaze to the Almendral area of Valparaiso, it was not only because of its status as one of the most prosperous areas of the city. The devastation there also highlighted the precariousness of construction on land gained from the sea, pointing to the dilemmas typical of a city with severe space limitations, built as it was in a narrow area between the Andes and the Pacific Ocean. Buenos Aires, on the other hand, was built at the edge of a vast, open plain. There, the catastrophe was understood and imagined as a result of an *absence* of variations in topography. We have seen how this feature was evoked by Brazilian correspondents, who contrasted this paucity of natural gifts with Rio's abundance. Bland topography was a crucial factor in the pictorial tradition of representations of the Pampas, in which artists attempting to portray it encountered a dearth of reference points that might allow for the construction of landscape.[141] This defining feature of the Pampas led to the cultivation of a news market with its own peculiarities, in which floods were a permanent item on the agenda of newspapers and magazines, and a presence in the photo-postcard trade.

Frequent floods would give rise to a vast archive of photographic images. In Buenos Aires, floods had the effect of drawing attention to some of the less manicured areas of town. Water was democratic, one journalist observed.[142] Postcards showed the inundated streets of the heavily Italian, working-class neighborhood of La Boca, filling the pages of newspapers and magazines and entering circulation in the market as "Souvenirs of Buenos Aires."

The "democratic" waters also drew the attention of the capital's press to surrounding towns, the future "Gran Buenos Aires", which seldomly appeared in newspapers and magazines. Similarly, the flood brought into view many far-flung towns of the Pampas, where seasonal rains would cause rivers and lakes to overflow. These young, thriving towns were the engine of the agro-export economy, and magnets for immigrants. Now, the walls and roofs of their newly constructed monuments of progress (the bank, the town hall, the main

---

[140] McCleary, "Inflaming the Fears of Theatergoers"; on the pedagogy of fire prevention in the carioca press, see de Souza, "Heróis das Chamas."

[141] Silvestri, *El lugar común*, pp. 67–70.   [142] *Caras y Caretas*, February 16, 1901.

Las inundaciones del domingo

EN EL OESTE DE LA CIUDAD

LA CALLE MINISTRO BRIN (BOCA)

Una creciente de nuestro río, inesperada como la resolución del doctor Quirno Costa en el asunto de las guías, produjo un avance de las aguas que llegaron á cubrir varias de las islas del Tigre, se encargaron de la limpieza municipal de las calles de San Fernando y en nuestra propia ciudad se adueñaron de diversos terrenos é hicieron su aparición en la Boca, Belgrano y Palermo, como en los mejores tiempos del siglo XIX. Para estos desbordamientos fluviales, lo propio que para la correspondiente acción de las autoridades edilicias, no existe la nueva centuria.

Las personas que se hallaban en las islas del Tigre, y vieron que la masa líquida, con verdadero espíritu democrático todo lo nivelaba con su caudal acuoso, hicieron uso inmediatamente de los botes para trasladarse á lugar menos expuesto al inmediato peligro de aaogarse y al más lejano de los dolores reumáticos.

En los pueblos antes citados el agua penetró en las casas, y los habitantes tuvieron que subirse á camas, armarios y mesas. En algunos edificios el agua alcanzó diferentes alturas, llegando hasta metro y medio del suelo. En el barrio de Tarupá, en el Tigre hubo que proceder

LA CALLE OLAVARRÍA (BOCA)

Image 14 *Caras y Caretas*, February 16, 1901

store) were seen emerging out of the muddy water.[143] Taken by residents in conjunction with the media in the capital, these photographs supported some important tropes of these communities' narrative: the pioneer's heroic struggle

---

[143] *Caras y Caretas*, March 24, 1900; April 21, 1900; September 2, 1899.

against nature's excesses, solidarity among neighbors, and – most of all – calls for aid from authorities in Buenos Aires. Not exactly catastrophes, these landscapes nevertheless highlighted the many vicissitudes of urbanization on the open plain.

Turning the page, moving from the latest photo of flooded streets to the special supplement on the earthquake, Valparaiso's sloping roads and views of the bay seen from the mountains were all that was needed to understand that these two disasters spoke of intense and contrasting urban experiences. Once again, the news intervened, solidifying differences, building an identity for the city "here," and sharpening the contrast with the city "over there."

4 The World That News Created

In South America's more modern societies, a chief form of knowledge about the world expanded at the turn of the twentieth century through international news. Judging by the diversity of publics and the size of the press markets, it was a widespread experience that touched a great majority of the urban population in one way or another – as readers, as consumers of images, as participants in casual conversation. Fragmented, sometimes confusing, always sensational, news had become a major vector of information, the most common way of access to what was far away.

Despite extreme distances from the main poles of information, the biggest and most cosmopolitan city in this region – Buenos Aires – was intensely connected. Its hybrid population of *criollos* and European immigrants was an avid consumer of contents from near and far. Concrete modes of access and reception of this heterogeneous trove of materials were heavily mediated by elements that composed a particular point of view – spatial distance, ethnic origin, cultural tradition, local conflict, among other factors. Far from diluting the main issues regarding the effects of news circulation, this singular perspective sheds light on several key trends of this widespread process. Let us turn now to the main features this picture reveals.

News opened a window onto distant cities, providing particular kinds of knowledge about them. The intrinsic connection between the press and the urban environment, coupled with the design of a transnational communication network that connected large cities with more intensity than rural areas or smaller towns, worked in that direction. So did the very logic of news selection, which placed news developed in large urban environments at the top of the hierarchy of priorities. Occasionally, a city would prepare itself to make news, deliberately turning into a spectacle for the benefit of the foreign press. Special correspondents were dispatched to the scene, providing insights and personal impressions about places that were more or less familiar to the reader. Most of the time, however, news triggered a discontinuous, contrasting set of scapes, the urban scenario functioning as a backdrop for a wide variety of content – wars, revolutions, state funerals, natural disasters – in an informative agenda with a growing bias toward the sensational. Thus, showcases and travel writing had to compete with many other forms of visibility, in which the focus was on something other than the city itself, yielding a more spontaneous and less controlled kind of exposure.

As a result of a combination of long-standing cultural ties, along with more recent shifts in power and demographics, the map drawn in Buenos Aires by turn-of-the-century news centered on a handful of Western European capitals. The geographical placement of correspondents speaks for itself in this regard. Concentrated in Paris, London, Madrid, Lisbon and Rome, they brought these cities ever closer to the reader. It was a proximity made of superimposed layers, where current events were interwoven with personal narratives about the fabric of social and cultural life in those places: accounts of strolls through the streets, out-of-the-way restaurants, literary gossip, theater openings, and even occasional glimpses into the underworld of crime and poverty. These cities were the implicit center of "the world", places so familiar that no particular introduction was deemed necessary.

The increased priority attached to news as an organizing principle fit into this configuration in several ways. On the one hand, it expanded the definition of Europe itself, making room for provincial cities and small towns where something sensational had happened. At the same time, the geography of wars would bring more Eastern European locations into view. Meanwhile, the news injected a powerful sense of synchrony with those places. Mediated by layers of local resignification, the acceleration brought about by the telegraph would have enormous repercussions for public opinion. The cycle of collective demonstrations triggered by the death of Umberto I occurred more than a decade ahead of the staggering response to the news of the outbreak of World War I, a landmark moment often pointed to as an indicator of the effects of cable technology in Latin American cities.[144]

On the other hand, a new horizon of references was opening up at the opposite end of the spectrum, one with more uneven chances of integration into a familiar framework. As in the many satires of the telegraph section, or the two *gauchos'* banter about the names of Russian cities that we met at the start, it was easy to find humor in the contrast between the distant and the near-at-hand, hinting at

---

[144] Sánchez, "Pasión de multitudes"; Winder, "Imagining World Citizenship in the Networked Newspaper."

the enormity of the expansion of references, as well as its limits. The evidence in this regard shows that the efficacy of news from afar did not depend on its actual distance but on how well and in what ways it lent itself to decoding upon reception. While news from Rome or Paris required little or no explanation, that coming out of, say, Beijing or Johannesburg was accompanied by any number of orienting devices that rarely broke the surface. Meanwhile, a revolution in faraway Saint Petersburg could find many points of contact and resonance with readers in Buenos Aires, infusing enticing views of the city with interpretation and commentary about its social life. Learning about the revolution, many saw this great capital for the first time, first through a museum-like display of postcard views, and then as the scene of a massive confrontation.

News functioned as an opportunity to educate readers about distant cities, as shown by the frequent combination of narratives of current events with an array of photo-postcards arranged like tourist trails. This juxtaposition of urgent content and urban still-life images typically took place at the beginning of a news cycle, and was often followed by photographic updates that were more in synch with the information. Overall, the oscillating, sometimes tense relationship between written and visual materials could be seen as another reminder of the burden of distance, the unavoidable discrepancy between the speed of telegraphic contents and that of their steam-correspondents and photographic counterparts. But one important result of this gap was the opportunity to activate vast archives of content, infusing previous street and building views with a new urgency. Thus, the news worked as the spark for a wealth of background information, the time-space gap filled with instructing or entertaining materials about faraway towns while the most relevant pictures and elaborate accounts made their way to the newsrooms.

As it displayed its repertoire of urban landmarks, the information network was also intervening in the regional map. The main effect was to bring closer those cities connected to the global transport and communications system, as can be seen from the everyday information flow between Buenos Aires and Rio de Janeiro, on the one hand, and Buenos Aires and Valparaiso-Santiago, on the other. This trans-urban (rather than transnational) space was shaped by its own dynamics, with Buenos Aires emerging as the dominant reference, along with a parallel and closely-knit network of exchange among ethnic and political communities on the Atlantic coast. An important by-product of this informational intimacy between capitals and main ports points to the construction of national identities. A comparative gaze evolved along the way, the regular dispatches of information giving rise to counterpoints where urban references seem to have heavily intervened in shaping notions about the character of entire neighboring nations.

The selective logic of visibility paid a price in implicit relative (or absolute) invisibilities. None was more obvious than that of certain older cities in the interior, places on the margins of this economic and cultural modernization, and farther away from the wide boulevards of the transmission networks. It was not just a question of infrastructure: sooner or later, all provincial cities gained access to the national telegraph and railway networks. But the triumph of certain criteria in judging what constituted "news" kept the focus on those points that formed the nexus of power and interaction with the world, as it was defined at the turn of the century. Occasionally, however, those same criteria of news worthiness would bring other towns to the forefront.

No matter how uneven, however, the world horizon created by the much-expanded access to international news was not one of pure Euro-centrism. If Paris remained very much at the core of the system of references, it is also true that the world in which this reference existed had become wider and more variegated. Such is the inescapable conclusion from the repertoire of information that was talked about and reacted to, which referred to very distant cities as well as those closer ones that had gained a more regular presence.

Equally clear is the imprint of local perspectives in the ways in which the many fragments of the world available to press readers were interpreted and appropriated, confirming the weight of this factor in any assessment of the global expansion of the news system. While new forms of access to information such as the submarine cable or the multiplication of correspondents brought with them the sense of a wider horizon, ultimately that possibility was shaped most decisively by the frames of meaning available (or eventually developed) at the point of reception. No matter how cosmopolitan Buenos Aires was, the type of cosmopolitism it produced was linked to a singular intersection of elements that was born locally. This does not necessarily mean that the impact was in direct proportion to the extent of previous knowledge: the dynamics of relevance were also a function of the elements involved in the story itself, and the avenues it opened for local translation. Whether comparing modernization programs, attempting to understand social and political conflicts, or trying to fathom the scale of natural disasters, the master key to interpretation was provided by the world at hand. Thus, the imagined *gauchos* of *PBT* could easily and quickly shift from the Winter Palace to the very *Porteño Revolución del Parque*, from snow-covered streets to that summer's political gossip, while at the same time commenting on the evocative sound of great Russian cities in the most vernacular Spanish. Everything, in the end, seemed to feed the machine of hybridization in a society still in full gestation.

Bibliography

Archives

Archives Nationales de France, Fonds Havas, 5 AR.

Newpapers and Periodicals

Argentine Republic, *Memoria del Ministerio del Interior*, 1900.

Caras y Caretas (Buenos Aires), 1898–1907.

Don Quixote (Buenos Aires), 1884.

El Mosquito (Buenos Aires), 1877.

Gazeta de Noticias (Rio de Janeiro), 1900–1902.

Jornal do Brazil (Rio de Janeiro), 1900, 1905.

La Ilustración Española y Americana (Madrid), 1880–1907.

La Ilustración Sud-Americana (Buenos Aires), 1892–1900.

La Nación (Buenos Aires), 1890–1907.

La Prensa (Buenos Aires), 1900, 1905, 1906.

La Protesta (Buenos Aires), 1900, 1905.

PBT (Buenos Aires), 1904–1907.

Union Postale Universelle, *Statistique Général, Service Postal publiées par le Bureau International* (Bern: Imprimerie Suter & Lierow, 1887–1900).

Books and Articles

AAVV, *Pasaje a Oriente. Narrativa de viajes de escritores argentinos. Selección y Prólogo de María Sonia Cristoff* (Buenos Aires: Fondo de Cultura Económica, 2009).

Ahvenainen, J., *The European Cable Companies in South America before the First World War* (Helsinki: Annals of the Finnish Academy of Science, 2004).

Albornoz, M., "O reino de Deus entre nós? Leituras de Lev Tolstoi na imprensa anarquista de Buenos Aires (1900–1910)" in A. Roberti (coord.), *Escritores & textos libertários* (Rio de Janeiro: FAPERJ / Ayran, 2020), pp. 27–56.

Albornoz, M., *Cuando el anarquismo causaba sensación. La sociedad argentina entre el miedo y la fascinación por los ideales libertarios* (Buenos Aires: Siglo XXI, 2021).

Albornoz, M., and Galeano, D., "Los agitadores móviles: trayectorias anarquistas y vigilancias portuarias en el Atlántico sudamericano, 1894–1908," *Almanack*, 21 (2019), 310–357.

Alexander, A. R., *City on Fire: Technology, Social Change and the Hazards of Progress in Mexico City, 1860–1910* (Pittsburgh: Pittsburgh University Press, 2016).

Appadurai, A., "Disjuncture and Difference in the Global Cultural Economy," *Theory, Culture, Society*, 7 (1990), 295–310.

Asseraf, A., *Electric News in Colonial Algeria* (Oxford: Oxford University Press, 2019).

Baggio, K. G., "Dos trópicos au Prata: viajantes brasileiros pela Argentina nas primeiras décadas do século XX," *História Revista* (UFG), 13: 1 (2008), 425–445.

Barbier, F., "Le commerce international de la librairie française au XIXe siècle (1815–1913)," *Revue d'histoire moderne et contemporaine*, 28: 1 (1981), 94–117.

Barbosa, M., *História Cultural da Imprensa. Brasil 1900–2000* (Rio de Janeiro: Mauad, 2007).

Barnhust, K. G., and Nerone, J., *The Form of News: A History* (New York/ London: The Guilford Press, 2001).

Barth, V., "Making the Wire Speak: Transnational Techniques of Journalism, 1860–1930" in M. Hampf and S. Müller-Pohl (eds.), *Global Communication Electric: Business, News and Politics in the World of Telegraphy* (Frankfurt/ New York: Campus Verlag, 2013), pp. 246–271.

Bell, D. "Cyborg Imperium, c. 1900" in A. Chapman and N. Chowe (eds.), *Coding and Representation from the Nineteenth Century to the Present: Scrambled Messages* (New York: Routledge, 2021).

Benjamin, W., "Paris, Capital of the Nineteenth Century" in Benjamin, *Reflections: Essays, Aphorisms, Autobiographical Writings*. Ed. and with an Introduction by Peter Demetz (New York: Schocken, 1986 [1938]), pp. 146–161.

Bergel, M., *El Oriente desplazado. Los intelectuales y los orígenes del tercermundismo en la Argentina* (Bernal, Argentina: UNQ, 2015).

Bergel, M., "En el país de los crisantemos. Enrique Gómez Carrillo y las derivas de la guerra ruso-japonesa en la prensa porteña," *Prismas. Revista de historia intelectual*, 25 (2021), forthcoming.

Blumenthal, E., *Exile and Nation-State Formation in Argentina and Chile, 1810–1862* (Cham, Switzerland: Palgrave Macmillan, 2019).

Boyd-Barrett, O., and Rantanen, T. (eds.), *The Globalization of News* (London: Sage, 1998).

Britton, J., *Cables, Crises and the Press: The Geopolitics of the New International Information System in the Americas, 1866–1903* (Albuquerque: University of New Mexico Press, 2013).

Britton, J., and Ahvenainen, J., "Showdown in South America: James Scrymser, John Pender, and United States–British Cable Competition," *The Business History Review*, 78: 1 (2004), 1–27.

Caimari, L., *Apenas un delincuente. Crimen, castigo y cultura en la Argentina moderna* (Buenos Aires: Siglo XXI, 2004).

Caimari, L., "De nuestro corresponsal exclusivo. Cobertura internacional y expansión informativa en los diarios de Buenos Aires de fines del siglo XIX," *Investigaciones y Ensayos*, 68 (2019), 23–53.

Caimari, L., "Derrotar la distancia. Articulación al mundo y políticas de la conexión en la Argentina, 1870s-1910s," *Estudios Sociales del Estado*, 5: 10 (2019), 128–167.

Caimari, L., "La carta y el paquete. Travesías de la palabra escrita entre Argentina y Chile a fines del siglo XIX," *Anuario Colombiano de Historia Social y de la Cultura*, 48: 2 (2021), 177–208.

Carey, J. W., *Communication as Culture: Essays on Media and Society* (Boston: Unwin Hyman, 1989).

Carey, J. W., "Technology and Ideology: The Case of the Telegraph" in Carey, *Communication as Culture: Essays on Media and Society*, rev. ed. (New York: Routledge, 2009), pp. 155–177.

Charle, C., *Le siècle de la presse (1830–1939)* (Paris: Seuil, 2004).

Chartier, R., "La conscience de la globalité. Commentaire," *Annales. Histoire, Sciences Sociales*, 56 (2001), 119–123.

Checa Godoy, A., *Historia de la prensa Iberoamericana* (Seville: Alfar, 1993).

Coelho de Souza Rodriguez, J. P., "Embaixadas originais: diplomacia, jornalismo e as relações Argentina-Brasil (1888–1935)," *Topoi (Rio J.)*, 18: 36 (2017), 537–562.

Conrad, S., Zimmermann, E., and Scarfi, J. P., "Latin America as a Laboratory: A Regional Case for Assessing the Potentialities and Limitations of Global History," *Población & Sociedad*, 28: 1 (2021), 228–244.

Cooper-Richet, D., "La presse hispanophone parisienne au XIX siècle: *El Correo de Ultramar* et les autres," *Çédille. Revista de estudios franceses*, 16 (2019): 81–100.

Darío, R., *España contemporánea* (Madrid: Mundo Latino, 1900).

De Luca, T. R., "Correspondente no Brasil. Origens da atividade nas décadas de 1870–1880," *Sur le journalisme, About journalism, Sobre jornalismo*, 5: 1 (2016). http://surlejournalisme.com/rev.

De Souza, V. L., "Heróis das Chamas. Uma análise dos ingressantes no Corpo de Bombeiros da cidade do Rio de Janeiro na Primeira República," unpublished PhD thesis, Pontificia Universidade Católica do Rio de Janeiro, mimeo.

De Vivo, F., "Microhistories of Long-Distance Information: Space, Movement and Agency in the Early Modern News," *Past and Present* (2019).

Desbordes, R. , "L'information internationale en Amérique du Sud: les agences et les réseaux *circa* 1874–1919," *Le Temps des Médias*, 20: 1 (2013), 125–138.

Desbordes, R., "Migrations and Information Networks in the 19th Century: Havas-Reuter Agencies in South America, 1874–1876," *Latin America History and Memory. Les Cahiers ALHIM*, 8 (2008).

Devoto, F., "La inmigración" in Academia Nacional de la Historia, *Nueva Historia de la Nación Argentina*, Vol. 4 (Buenos Aires: Planeta, 2000), pp. 77–107.

Di Pietro, S., and Tófalo, A., *La situación educativa a través de los censos de población* (Buenos Aires: Ministerio de Educación de la Ciudad, 2013).

Dias, A., *Do Rio a Buenos Aires, episódios e impressões d'uma viagem* (Rio de Janeiro: Imprensa Nacional, 1901).

Eleutério, M. de L., "Imprensa a serviço de progresso" in A. L. Martins and T. R. de Luca (orgs.), *História de imprensa no Brasil* (São Paulo: Contextos, 2008), pp. 83–101.

Fernández, P., "El monopolio del mercado internacional de impresos en castellano en el siglo XIX: Francia, España y 'la ruta' de Hispanoamérica," *Bulletin Hispanique*, 100: 1 (1998), 165–190.

Feyel, G., "Les transformations technologiques de la presse au XIXe siècle" in D. Kalifa et al. (dirs.), *La civilisation du journal. Histoire culturelle et littéraire de la presse française au XIXe siècle* (Paris: Nouveau Monde, 2011), pp. 127–139.

Franco, M., "El estado de excepción a comienzos del siglo XX: de la cuestión obrera a la cuestión nacional," *Avances del Cesor*, 16: 20 (2019), 29–51.

Frisby, D., *Cityscapes of Modernity: Critical Explorations* (Cambridge, UK: Polity Press, 2007).

Fritsche, P., *Reading Berlin 1900* (Cambridge, MA: Harvard University Press, 1996).

Galante, J., "Distant Loyalties: World War I and the Italian Atlantic," unpublished PhD thesis, Pittsburgh University, 2016.

Gayol, S., "La unanimidad de la congoja: la muerte de Eva Perón en 1952" in S. Gayol and S. Palermo (eds.), *Política y cultura de masas en la Argentina de la primera mitad del siglo XX* (Los Polvorines: UNGS, 2018), pp. 289–313.

Gené, M., and Szir, S. (eds.), *A vuelta de página. Usos del impreso ilustrado en Buenos Aires, siglos XIX y XX* (Buenos Aires: Edhasa, 2018).

Giddens, A., *The Consequences of Modernity* (Stanford, CA: Stanford University Press, 1990).

Gobello, J., *Blanqueo etimológico del Lunfardo* (Buenos Aires: Dunken, 2005).

Goebel, M., *Overlapping Geographies of Belonging: Migrations, Regions, and Nations in the Western South Atlantic* (Washington, DC: American Historical Association, 2013).

Goldgel, V., *Cuando lo nuevo conquistó América* (Buenos Aires: Siglo XXI, 2013).

Gómez Carrillo, E., *La Rusia actual* (Paris: Garnier, 1906).

Gorelik, A., *La grilla y el parque. Espacio público y cultura urbana en Buenos Aires, 1887–1936* (Bernal, Argentina: Universidad de Quilmes, 1998).

Guarneri, J., *Newsprint Metropolis: City Papers and the Making of Modern Americans* (Chicago: University of Chicago Press, 2017).

Guimarães, V., "From Liner to Telegraph: The Foreign Popular Press in Brazil at the Turn of the Twentieth Century" in D. Cooper-Richet and J.-Y. Mollier (orgs.), *Le commerce transatlantique de la librairie, un des fondements de la mondialisation culturelle (France-Portugal-Brazil, XVIIIe–XIXe siècle)* (Campinas SP, Brazil: Publiel, 2012), pp. 149–162.

Halperin Donghi, T., *The Contemporary History of Latin America* (Durham, NC: Duke University Press, 1993).

Headrick, D., *The Invisible Weapon: Telecommunications and International Politics* (Oxford: Oxford University Press, 1991).

Healey, M., *The Ruins of the New Argentina: Peronism and the Remaking of San Juan in the 1944 Earthquake* (Durham, NC: Duke University Press, 2011).

Hevia, J. L., "Looting and Its Discontents: Moral Discourse and the Plundering of Beijing" in R. Bickers and R. G. Tiedemann (eds.), *The Boxers, China, and the World* (Lanham, MD: Rowman & Littlefield, 2007), pp. 93–114.

Hubert, R., "Sinology on the Edge: Borges' Reviews of Chinese Literature (1937–1942)," *Variaciones Borges*, 39 (2015), 81–101.

Jaksic, I., "Disciplinas y temáticas de la intelectualidad chilena en el siglo XIX" in I. Jaksic and S. Gazmuri (eds.), *Intelectuales y pensamiento político (Historia política de Chile, 1810–2010)*, Vol. IV (Santiago de Chile: Fondo de Cultura Económica, 2018).

Kalifa, D., *L'encre et le sang* (Paris: Fayard, 1995).

Kalifa, D., et al. (dirs.), *La civilisation du journal. Histoire culturelle et littéraire de la presse française au XIXe siècle* (Paris: Nouveau Monde, 2011).

Lobato, M. Z., *Prensa obrera. Buenos Aires y Montevideo 1890–1958* (Buenos Aires: Edhasa, 2009).

López, A., "Early Cinema and Modernity in Latin America," *Cinema Journal*, 40: 1 (2000), 48–78.

Malisheva, G., and Noussinova, N., "Actualités et fausses actualités chez Pathé. La guerre russo-japonaise, 1904–1905" in M. Marie and L. Le Forestier (dirs.), *La Firme Pathé Frères* (Paris: AFRHC, 2004).

Martínez Gutiérrez, E., "Donde la ciudad se escribe. Prensa, urbanización y cultura en Robert E. Park," Oʙᴇᴛs. *Revista de Ciencias Sociales*, 11: 2 (2016), 487–512.

Martland, S., *Construir Valparaíso. Tecnología, municipalidad y Estado, 1820–1920* (Santiago de Chile: Dirección de Bibliotecas, Archivos y Museos/ Centro de Investigaciones Diego Barros Arana, 2017).

Martland, S., "Reconstructing the City, Constructing the State: Government in Valparaíso after the Earthquake of 1906," *Hispanic American Historical Review*, 87: 2 (2007), 221–254.

McCleary, K., "Inflaming the Fears of Theatergoers: How Fires Shaped the Public Sphere in Buenos Aires, Argentina, 1880–1910" in S. Pyne, J. Sand, G. Bankoff and U. Lubken (eds.), *Flammable Cities: Urban Conflagration and the Making of the Modern World* (Madison: University of Wisconsin Press, 2012), pp. 254–272.

Mollier, J.-Y., "Introduction" in D. Cooper-Richet and J.-Y. Mollier (orgs.), *Le commerce transatlantique de la librairie, un des fondements de la mondialisation culturelle (France-Portugal-Brazil, XVIIIe–XIXe siècle)* (Campinas SP, Brazil: Publiel, 2012) pp. 9–16.

Moya, J., "Migration and the Historical Formation of Latin America in a Global Perspective," *Sociologías*, Porto Alegre, 20: 49 (2018), 24–68.

Muhlmann, G., and Plenel, E. (eds.), *Le journaliste et le sociologue. Robert E. Park* (Paris: Médiateque, 2008).

Müller, S., "From Cabling the Atlantic to Wiring the World: A Review Essay on the 150th Anniversary of the Atlantic Telegraph Cable of 1866," *Technology and Culture*, 57: 3 (2017), 507–526.

Müller, S., *Wiring the World: The Social and Cultural Creation of Global Telegraph Networks* (New York: Columbia University Press, 2016).

Navarro Viola, J., *Anuario de la prensa argentina* (Buenos Aires: Imprenta Coni e Hijos, 1897).

Needell, J., *Belle époque tropical. Sociedad y cultura de élite en Río de Janeiro a fines del siglo XIX y principios del XX* (Bernal, Argentina: Universidad Nacional de Quilmes, 2012).

Nikkles, D. P., *Under the Wire: How the Telegraph Changed Diplomacy* (Cambridge, MA: Harvard University Press, 2003).

Ojeda, A., *La incorporación sistemática de la imagen visual a la prensa diaria argentina. El caso paradigmático del diario* La Nación *entre 1894 y 1904*, PhD thesis, Universidad Nacional de La Plata (Argentina), 2016.

Osterhammel, J., *The Transformation of the World: A Global History of the Nineteenth Century* (Princeton, NJ: Princeton University Press, 2014).

Palmer, P., *Des petits journaux aux grandes agences* (Paris: Aubier, 1983).

Park, R., "News as a Form of Knowledge: A Chapter in the Sociology of Knowledge," *American Journal of Sociology*, 45: 5 (1940), 669–686.

Preuss, O., *Transnational South America: Experiences, Ideas, and Identities, 1860–1900s* (New York: Routledge, 2016).

Pyne, S., *Fire: A Brief History* (Seattle: University of Washington Press, 2001).

Pyne, S., Sand, J., Bankoff, G., and Lubken, U. (eds.), *Flammable Cities: Urban Conflagration and the Making of the Modern World* (Madison: University of Wisconsin Press, 2012).

Rantanen, T., "The New Sense of Place in 19th Century News," *Media, Culture & Society*, 25: 4 (2003), 435–449.

Reggini, H., *Sarmiento y las telecomunicaciones. La obsesión del hilo* (Buenos Aires: Galápagos, 1997).

Rogers, G., *Caras y Caretas. Cultura, política y espectáculo en los inicios del siglo XX argentino* (La Plata, Argentina: Editorial de la Universidad Nacional de La Plata, 2008).

Roman, C., "La modernización de la prensa periódica, entre *La Patria Argentina* (1879) y *Caras y Caretas* (1898)" in A. Laera (dir.), *El brote de los géneros* (vol. 3, *Historia crítica de la literatura argentina*) (Buenos Aires: Emecé, 2010), pp. 15–38.

Roman, C., *Prensa, política y cultura visual. El Mosquito (Buenos Aires, 1863–1893)* (Buenos Aires: Ampersand, 2017).

Romano, E., *Revolución en la lectura. El discurso periodístico-literario en las primeras revistas ilustradas rioplatenses* (Buenos Aires: Catálogos-El Calafate, 2004).

Romero, J. L., *Latinoamérica. Las ciudades y las ideas* (Buenos Aires: Siglo XXI, 1976).

Romero, J. L., "La ciudad burguesa" in J. L. Romero and L. A. Romero (dirs.), *Buenos Aires. Historia de cuatro siglos*, vol. 2 (Buenos Aires: Altamira, 2000), pp. 9–17.

Rosario Hubert, *Disorientations. Latin American Fictions of East Asia*, Doctoral Dissertation, Harvard University, 2014.

Rowley, A., *Open Letters: Russian Popular Culture and the Picture Postcard, 1880–1922* (Toronto: University of Toronto Press, 2013).

Rozeaux, S., "Être correspondant de la presse brésilienne en Europe: anatomie sociale et circulation d'un nouvel acteur du paysage médiatique dans l'espace atlantique," *Actes du colloque Médias 19: "Les journalistes: identités et modernités,"* 2017.

Sánchez, E., "Pasión de multitudes: la prensa y la opinión pública de Buenos Aires frente al estallido de la Gran Guerra," *Anuario del IEHS*, 33: 1 (2018), 177–204.

Sarmiento, D. F., *Obras Completas. Vol X: Legislación y progresos en Chile* (Buenos Aires: Imprenta y Litografía "Mariano Moreno," 1896).

Schudson, M., *Discovering the News: A Social History of American Newspapers* (New York: Basic Books, 1978).

Schwartz, V. (ed.), *Cinema and the Invention of Modern Life* (Berkeley: University of California Press, 1995).

Serulnikov, S., "El secreto del mundo. Sobre historias globales y locales en América Latina," *História da Historiografia*, 13: 32 (2020), 147–184.

Servelli, M., *A través de la República. Corresponsales-viajeros en la prensa de entresiglos (XIX_XX)* (Buenos Aires: Prometeo, 2018).

Silberstein-Loeb, J., *The International Distribution of News: The Associated Press, Press Association, and Reuters, 1848–1947* (Cambridge: Cambridge University Press, 2014).

Silvestri, G., *El lugar común. Una historia de las figuras de paisaje en el Río de la Plata* (Buenos Aires: Edhasa, 2011).

Simmel, G., "The Metropolis and Mental Life" in *The Sociology of Georg Simmel*, trans. and ed. K. H. Wolff (Glencoe, IL: Free Press, 1950), pp. 409–424.

Singer, B., *Melodrama and Modernity: Early Sensational Cinema and Its Contexts* (New York: Columbia University Press, 2001).

Singer, B., "Modernity, Hyperstimulus, and the Rise of Popular Sensationalism" in L. Charney and V. Schwartz (eds.), *Cinema and the Invention of Modern Life* (Berkeley: University of California Press, 1995).

Siskind, M., *Cosmopolitan Desires: Global Modernity and World Literatura in Latin America* (Evanston, IL: Northwestern University Press, 2014).

Skidmore, T., *Black into White: Race and Nationality in Brasilian Thought* (Durham, NC: Duke University Press, 1993).

Sodré, N. W., *A história da imprensa no Brasil* (Rio de Janeiro: Civilização Brasileira, 1966).

Szir, S., "El semanario popular ilustrado *Caras y Caretas* y las transformaciones del paisaje cultural de la modernidad. Buenos Aires, 1898–1908," unpublished PhD thesis, University of Buenos Aires, 2011.

Szir, S., "Entre el arte y la cultura masiva. Las ilustraciones de la ficción literaria en Caras *y Caretas* (1898–1908)" in L. Malosetti and M. Gené (comps.), *Impresiones porteñas. Imagen y palabra en la historia cultural de Buenos Aires* (Buenos Aires: Edhasa, 2009), pp. 109–139.

Szir, S., "Reporte documental, régimen visual y fotoperiodismo. La ilustración de noticias en la prensa periódica de Buenos Aires," *Caiana*, 3 (2013), 1–16.

Taboada, H., "Un orientalismo periférico: viajeros latinoamericanos 1786–1920," *Estudios de Asia y África*, 106 (1998) 285–305.

Tell, V., *El lado visible. Fotografía y progreso en la Argentina a fines del siglo XIX* (Buenos Aires: Unsam, 2017).

Tell, V., "Reproducción fotográfica e impresión fotomecánica: materialidad y apropiación de imágenes a finales del siglo XIX" in L. Malosetti and M. Gené (comps.), *Impresiones porteñas. Imagen y palabra en la historia cultural de Buenos Aires* (Buenos Aires: Edhasa, 2009), pp. 141–163.

Thérenty, M., and Vaillant, A. (dirs.), *Presse, nations et mondialisation au xixe siècle* (Paris: Nouveau Monde Éditions, 2010).

Weber, J. I., "Elenco de publicaciones periódicas italianas de Buenos Aires (1854–1910)," *AdVersus*, V: 34 (2018), 124–189.

Wenzlhuemer, R., *Connecting the Nineteenth-Century World: The Telegraph and Globalization* (Cambridge: Cambridge University Press, 2013).

Winder, G., "Imagining World Citizenship in the Networked Newspaper: La Nación Reports the Assassination at Sarajevo, 1914," *Historical Social Research / Historische Sozialforschung*, 35: 1 (2010), 140–166.

Winder, G., "Telecommunications Technology and News of Disaster: Earthquake Reporting in the Los Angeles Times, 1917–1939" in M. Hampf and S. Müller-Pohl, *Global Communication Electric: Business, News and Politics in the World of Telegraphy* (Frankfurt/New York: Campus Verlag, 2013), pp. 275–301.

Winseck, D., and Pike, R., *Communication and Empire: Media, Markets, and Globalization, 1860–1930* (Durham, NC: Duke University Press, 2007).

Cambridge Elements

Global Urban History

Michael Goebel
Graduate Institute Geneva

Michael Goebel is the Pierre du Bois Chair Europe and the World and Associate Professor of International History at the Graduate Institute Geneva. His research focuses on the histories of nationalism, of cities, and of migration. He is the author of *Anti-Imperial Metropolis: Interwar Paris and the Seeds of Third World Nationalism* (2015).

Tracy Neumann
Wayne State University

Tracy Neumann is an Associate Professor of History at Wayne State University. Her research focuses on global and transnational approaches to cities and the built environment. She is the author of *Remaking the Rust Belt: The Postindustrial Transformation of North America* (2016) and of essays on urban history and public policy.

Joseph Ben Prestel
Freie Universität Berlin

Joseph Ben Prestel is an Assistant Professor (wissenschaftlicher Mitarbeiter) of History at Freie Universität Berlin. His research focuses on the histories of Europe and the Middle East in the nineteenth and twentieth centuries as well as on global and urban history. He is the author of *Emotional Cities: Debates on Urban Change in Berlin and Cairo, 1860–1910* (2017).

About the Series

This series proposes a new understanding of urban history by reinterpreting the history of the world's cities. While urban history has tended to produce single-city case studies, global history has mostly been concerned with the interconnectedness of the world. Combining these two approaches produces a new framework to think about the urban past. The individual titles in the series emphasize global, comparative, and transnational approaches. They deliver empirical research about specific cities, while also exploring questions that expand the narrative outside the immediate locale to give insights into global trends and conceptual debates. Authored by established and emerging scholars whose work represents the most exciting new directions in urban history, this series makes pioneering research accessible to specialists and non-specialists alike.

Printed in the United States
by Baker & Taylor Publisher Services